The Essentials of Special Education Law

Special Education Law, Policy, and Practice

Series Editors: Mitchell Yell, PhD, University of South Carolina, and David Bateman, PhD, Shippensburg University of Pennsylvania

The *Special Education Law, Policy, and Practice* series highlights current trends and legal issues in the education of students with disabilities. The books in this series link legal requirements with evidence-based instruction and highlight practical applications for working with students with disabilities. The titles in the *Special Education Law, Policy, and Practices* series are designed not only to be required textbooks for general education and special education preservice teacher education programs but are also designed for practicing teachers, education administrators, principals, school counselors, school psychologists, parents, and others interested in improving the lives of students with disabilities. The *Special Education Law, Policy, and Practice* series is committed to research-based practices working to provide appropriate and meaningful educational programming for students with disabilities and their families.

Titles in Series

The Essentials of Special Education Law

Andrew M. Markelz
Ball State University

David F. Bateman
Shippensburg University

ROWMAN & LITTLEFIELD
Lanham • Boulder • New York • London

Acquisitions Editor: Mark Kerr
Assistant Editor: Courtney Packard
Sales and Marketing Inquiries: textbooks@rowman.com

Credits and acknowledgments for material borrowed from other sources, and reproduced with permission, appear on the appropriate pages within the text.

Published by Rowman & Littlefield
An imprint of The Rowman & Littlefield Publishing Group, Inc.
4501 Forbes Boulevard, Suite 200, Lanham, Maryland 20706
www.rowman.com

6 Tinworth Street, London SE11 5AL, United Kingdom

British Library Cataloguing in Publication Information Available

Library of Congress Cataloging-in-Publication Data

Names: Markelz, Andrew M., 1980– author. | Bateman, David, 1963– author.
Title: The essentials of Special Education Law / Andrew M. Markelz and David F. Bateman.
Description: Lanham, Maryland : Rowman & Littlefield, [2021] | Series: Special education law, policy, and practice | Includes bibliographical references and index
Identifiers: LCCN 2021015943 (print) | LCCN 2021015944 (ebook) |
    ISBN 9781538150023 (cloth) | ISBN 9781538150030 (paperback) |
    ISBN 9781538150047 (epub)
Subjects: LCSH: Special education—Law and legislation—United States.
Classification: LCC KF4209.3 .B3738 2021 (print) | LCC KF4209.3 (ebook) |
    DDC 344.73/0791—dc23
LC record available at https://lccn.loc.gov/2021015943
LC ebook record available at https://lccn.loc.gov/2021015944

♾™ The paper used in this publication meets the minimum requirements of American National Standard for Information Sciences—Permanence of Paper for Printed Library Materials, ANSI/NISO Z39.48-1992.

Contents

Preface

Special education law is a topic of great importance to educators, administrators, and families. We wrote this book to be a valuable contribution to teacher preparation programs as well as professionals in the field. The vast majority of undergraduate teacher preparation programs do not have a course dedicated to special education law. Oftentimes, topics of law are overlooked or irregularly interwoven into courses based on individual instructors' decisions. Current special education law textbooks target graduate-level courses and are too extensive for supplemental text adoption at the undergraduate level. Our book is an ideal supplemental textbook that any undergraduate course can adopt for a more systematic coverage of what is truly essential about special education law for teachers and administrators. We wrote this book to cut through the complexities of legal jargon, legislation, regulation, and case law. *The Essentials of Special Education* is a concise yet comprehensive resource for understanding special education law.

The first section of our book covers the role of government in establishing and defining special education. Seminal court cases and legislative initiatives that have shaped the field of special education are explored to provide historical context for understanding special education today. The second section examines each of the six pillars of the Individuals with Disabilities Education Act of 2004. Key court cases that have influenced each pillar are presented along with practical tips for legally compliant implementation. The third section covers important topics that every special educator must be familiar with such as discipline, confidentiality, and transition services. Throughout each chapter, key terms are highlighted along with questions to foster in-depth classroom discussions.

We hope our book serves as a valuable resource for educators, administrators, and families. Special education law may seem intimidating at first; however, once the essential components and relationships of legislation, regulation, and case law are understood, anybody can have a strong foundation to make legally justifiable decisions. As you will soon read, the evolution of special education trends in a hopeful direction; however, the progress made has not been a foregone conclusion. Knowing and applying special education law continue to advance the rights of students with disabilities through effort and advocacy.

PART I

Role of Government

CHAPTER 1

The Government and Special Education

> *As special education teachers we are not simply recipients of the law; we can actively engage in shaping legislation. The first step to bringing about change is to understand how government works.*
>
> Dr. Sarah Nagro
> George Mason University

The government of the United States is a federal system composed of a union of state governments and a centralized federal government. The separation of powers between the federal government and state governments is delineated in the U.S. Constitution which was signed in 1787 after the Revolutionary War and ratified by the first thirteen states. The U.S. Constitution is the foundational source of law in the United States. The U.S. Constitution delegates powers and responsibilities between three branches of government while also delineating powers to the states. In particular, the Tenth Amendment articulates that all powers not identified in the U.S. Constitution are granted to the states (figure 1.1). Through an interaction of laws, regulations, and judicial interpretations, the U.S. government has played a critical role in the emergence of special education for students with disabilities. In this chapter we will discuss the basics of the U.S. federal government and answer these essential questions:

1. What are the three branches of government?
2. What are the four sources of law?
3. How do the three branches of government influence special education?
4. Where can I find more information on the three branches of government?

> *The powers not delegated to the United States by the Constitution, not prohibited by it to the States, are reserved to the States respectively, or to the people.*

Figure 1.1 Tenth Amendment of the U.S. Constitution.

What are the three branches of government?

After fighting for independence from a monarchy (i.e., a king), the **founders** sought to prevent a singular controlling authority from harnessing too much power.

To achieve this, the U.S. Constitution divides the federal government into three branches to make sure no individual or group will have too much power. Within the articles of the Constitution, the particular responsibilities of each branch and its oversight abilities on the other branches are established.

The Legislative Branch

The legislative branch, also called Congress, is responsible for creating laws. Congress has committees that have expertise in specific areas of legislation, and through **parliamentary procedures** it drafts legislation, debates the legislation, then votes to approve or disprove the legislation.

Congress was established to create laws and closely represent the will of the people of each state within the federal government. To do so, Congress is composed of two bodies: the Senate and the House of Representatives. A piece of legislation must pass both the Senate and House of Representatives before it can become law.

The Senate. There are two elected senators from each state, totaling 100 senators. A senate term is six years and there is no limit on the number of terms a senator can serve. Senators are elected by and represent the **constituents** of their entire state; therefore, each senator must consider the political desires of all people within their state when they propose and vote on legislation.

Senators do have the flexibility to take more politically controversial votes because a six-year term provides time between elections for them to explain and defend votes. The Senate is considered the body within Congress that slowly and meticulously, sometimes obstructively, debates legislation.

The House of Representatives. The House of Representatives is comprised of 435 representatives from each state who represent a portion of their state, known as a Congressional District. Congressional Districts average nearly 750,000 people (Desilver, 2018). Therefore, more populated states have more representatives than less populated states. A representative term is two years with no limit on the number of terms. This quicker election cycle requires representatives to be much more responsive to their constituents' political wills.

Furthermore, Congressional Districts tend to be more politically homogenous which creates representatives with stronger ideological positions as opposed to senators who attempt to represent a wider spectrum of political ideology. The House of Representatives is considered the body within Congress that is more responsive to the shifting political winds of their constituents and that rapidly proposes legislation accordingly.

The Executive Branch

At the top of the executive branch is the president of the United States. In tandem with the president's role as the commander-in-chief of the military, the executive branch, as identified in Article II of the U.S. Constitution, is responsible for executing laws passed by Congress. In other words, the executive branch is charged with enforcing and regulating laws. To help the president accomplish this task, they have a cabinet of advisers and department secretaries who oversee specific areas of the executive branch and assist the president and vice president in carrying out their agenda and enforcing the law. Figure 1.2 is a list of departments within the president's cabinet.

Each department is an extensive organization with a hierarchical structure of authority and thousands of employees, sometimes millions of employees (e.g., the Department of Defense). Laws that are passed by Congress are often written with vague language and never describe how the new law should be implemented. Therefore, it is up to the executive branch to explain the implications of the new law and provide guidance on how to implement it. For example, when the Every Student Succeeds Act of 2015 (discussed in chapter 2) was passed by Congress and signed into law by President Obama, it became the responsibility of the Department of Education to disseminate the information to state governments and school officials of how the new law changed requirements that were previously the law under the No Child Left Behind Act of 2001.

Sometimes federal laws are comprehensive, changes to previous policy are extensive, and a vast number of Americans are affected. Other times, laws might be more specific and only affect a small industry or particular group.

U.S. Department of Agriculture	U.S. Department of Commerce
U.S. Department of Defense	U.S. Department of Education
U.S. Department of Energy	U.S. Department of Health and Human Services
U.S. Department of Homeland Security	U.S. Department of Housing
U.S. Department of Justice	U.S. Department of Labor
U.S. Department of State	U.S. Department of the Interior
U.S. Department of Treasury	U.S. Department of Transportation
U.S. Department of Veterans Affairs	

Figure 1.2   List of 15 Departments within the President's Cabinet.

Either way, the executive branch is responsible for taking new laws passed by Congress and ensuring those laws are applied and followed.

The Judicial Branch

The judicial branch interprets the meaning of laws, applies laws to individual cases, and decides if laws violate the Constitution. Often, the vague language in legislation creates confusion among those who are charged with implementing the law. The judicial branch acts as a referee to clarify the meaning of laws and settle disputes between **plaintiffs** and **defendants** of lawsuits.

Since the U.S. Constitution is the foundational source of law, no legislative branch law or executive branch policy can violate the Constitution. Per Article III of the Constitution, the judicial branch is tasked with making these judgments. The president nominates judges to serve lifetime appointments and Congress votes as to whether nominees can serve or not. The judicial branch is comprised of nearly 100 U.S. District Courts, 13 U.S. Courts of Appeals, and the Supreme Court.

Three tiers of authoritative hierarchy exist among courts, both at the state and federal government level. The structure of this hierarchy is similar between states and the federal courts; therefore, we will focus on the federal courts. A **trial court** (i.e., a U.S. District Court) is the level at which the fact-finding process takes place, except for in special education matters where a due process hearing officer is the fact-finder.

A judge and jury hear the facts of the dispute, then the jury provides a verdict based on the strength of the plaintiff's or defendant's case. U.S. District Courts have **jurisdiction** over states based on geographical distribution.

If a plaintiff or defendant loses a case at the trial court level, they typically have the right to appeal the court's decision to a **Court of Appeals** (i.e., a U.S. Circuit Court of Appeals).

Because the facts of a case have already been established at the trial court level, Courts of Appeals do not have juries. Rather, three judges read written briefs and hear oral arguments from lawyers about whether the lower court's ruling should be affirmed, reversed, or modified. Judges' decisions are based on whether principles of the law were applied correctly. The geographical jurisdictions of the thirteen U.S. Courts of Appeals are shown in figure 1.3 and listed in table 1.1.

The court of last resort and the highest court in the United States is called the U.S. Supreme Court (remember, states have a similar structure of state-level trial courts, state-level appeal courts, and state-level supreme courts). The U.S. Supreme Court has nine justices. The U.S. Supreme Court receives hundreds of requests but only hears a small number of cases, less than 1 percent of petitions filed (United States Courts, n.d.). The Court only agrees to hear cases concerning important questions about constitutional or federal law or to resolve issues that have split circuit courts with contradictory rulings. Figure 1.4 outlines the compositions and roles of the three branches of government.

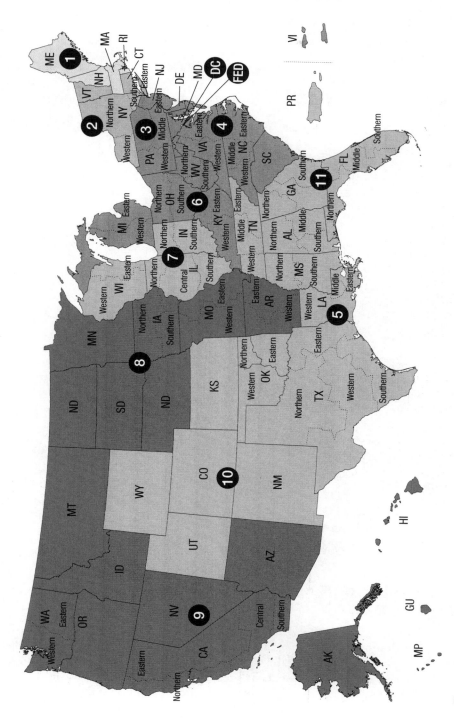

Figure 1.3 Geographic Boundaries of U.S. Courts of Appeals and U.S. District Courts.

TABLE 1.1 The U.S. Circuit Courts of Appeal

1st	2nd	3rd	4th	5th	6th	7th	8th	9th	10th	11th	12th	13th
ME	CT	DE	MD	LA	KY	IL	AR	AK	CO	AL	DC	FED
MA	NY	NJ	SC	MS	OH	IN	IA	AZ	KS	GA		
NH	VT	PA	NC	TX	MI	WI	MN	CA	NM	FL		
RI			VA		TN		MO	HI	OK			
		WV					NE	ID	UT			
							ND	MT	WY			
							SD	NV				
								OR				
								WA				

Note: The 13th Circuit is called the Federal Circuit and hears appeals on specialized topics (e.g., patents, trade).

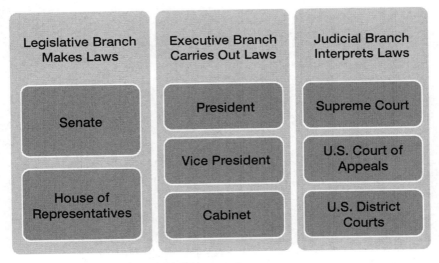

Figure 1.4 The Three Branches of Government.

What are the four sources of law?
The U.S. Constitution

As previously mentioned, the U.S. Constitution is the primary source of law. The Constitution (a) outlines fundamental rules in how the U.S. federal system of democracy functions, (b) establishes boundaries for governmental action, and (c) designates authority, responsibilities, and separation of power among the three branches of government (Berring & Edinger, 2005). Provisions in the U.S. Constitution allow the federal government to create federal laws. For example, Article I, Section 8 of the U.S. Constitution authorizes Congress to spend money to provide for general welfare. Described in the Constitution is a procedure for Congress and the states to amend the Constitution, which is not easy and has only been done twenty-seven times. Soon after the U.S. Constitution was adopted by the first states, ten amendments, known as the Bill of Rights, were adopted in 1791 to describe the basic rights of individuals.

It was not until after the Civil War that the Fourteenth Amendment was adopted. The Fourteenth Amendment, which would become a very consequential amendment for special education, states:

> All persons born or naturalized in the United States and subject to the jurisdiction thereof, are citizens of the United States and of the State wherein they reside. No State shall make or enforce any law which shall abridge the privileges or immunities of citizens of the United States; nor shall any State deprive any person of life, liberty, or property, without due process of law; nor deny to any person within its jurisdiction the equal protection of the laws.

All fifty states have their own state constitutions which describe the power and authority of state branches of government, such as a legislative branch (legislature), an executive branch (governor), and a court system. State constitutions are more detailed than the U.S. Constitution as these documents detail day-to-day operations of state governments. States can provide additional rights to individuals that are not found in the U.S. Constitution; however, states cannot deny rights found in the U.S. Constitution (Yell, 2019).

Statutory Law

When one thinks of laws, they probably think of statutory laws. Statutory laws are laws passed by the legislative branch (Congress). The U.S. Constitution delegates authority to Congress to make statutes (i.e., laws). The process of a bill becoming a law is long and complicated. In the end, however, each chamber in the legislative branch (the Senate and House of Representatives) must agree on the details of the bill. Then, each chamber must vote by a majority to pass the bill. The bill is then sent to the president to sign or **veto**. If the president signs the bill, it becomes a law. If the president vetoes the bill, the legislative branch can override the veto by a two-thirds majority in each chamber.

Regulatory Law

Once a law is passed, it needs to be carried out. The executive branch is charged, per the U.S. Constitution, to execute and enforce laws. Oftentimes, statutes passed by Congress are broad and lack details. To help fill in the details, Congress allows the appropriate executive branch agency to develop regulations.

These **regulations** will assist those impacted by the law in knowing how to implement and enforce it. Depending on who is affected by the new law, one of the fifteen departments within the executive branch cabinet will serve as the entity responsible for providing specifics to the general content of the law. For example, any law that is passed concerning education will become the responsibility of the Department of Education. Within the Department of Education are numerous agencies with areas of expertise. The employees within each agency are tasked with disseminating information about the new law to relevant stakeholders, providing guidance on how to implement the law, and what happens for violating the new law. All this information is called regulatory law, and regulatory law has the same force as statutory law.

Case Law

Another source of law is called case law. A case law is established when judges publish legal opinions following a decision on a court case that involved the interpretation of statutes, regulations, or U.S. Constitutional matters. Remember, the judicial branch is responsible for interpreting laws. Therefore, when conflict arises between two parties about a law, judges rule to settle the dispute. These rulings carry authority and establish **legal precedent**.

The U.S. court system is based on legal precedent, meaning once a legal principle has been established, it is applied to other cases with similar facts. The tiers of authority, and the jurisdiction courts have, play an important role in legal precedent.

Courts have **controlling authority** over courts that fall under their jurisdiction. For example, the Fifth Circuit Court of Appeals has jurisdiction over every lower court in the states of Texas, Mississippi, and Louisiana. When the Fifth Circuit Court makes a ruling, that ruling has controlling authority over all courts within those three states. Those lower courts must adhere to the Circuit Court's legal interpretation and apply that interpretation in cases with similar facts. The Fifth Circuit Court, however, does not have controlling authority over the Seventh Circuit Court's jurisdiction. But courts not under the jurisdiction of other courts do have **persuasive authority**.

Let's say the Fifth Circuit Court heard a case about providing special education services to a student with autism and ruled in favor of the student. A year later, a case with similar facts involving a disagreement about the same law is argued in the Seventh Circuit Court. The Seventh Circuit Court does not have to follow the ruling of the Fifth Circuit Court but can read the published opinion of those judges and be persuaded by their legal rationale to rule similarly. The strength of a court's legal rationale and justification for interpreting a law can persuade other courts to adopt their rationale and justification.

The U.S. Supreme Court is the highest court and has the ultimate controlling authority. When the U.S. Supreme Court makes a decision, all fifty states must adhere to the ruling and apply the legal precedent in all similar cases. Since there are nine justices on the Supreme Court, a majority of five justices is needed to decide a case. In lower courts with only three judges, a majority of two is needed. Typically, one judge is selected to write the opinion of the court which states the ruling and the reasoning for arriving at that decision. If there are judges in the minority, a dissenting opinion is written which states the reason for disagreeing with the majority. Dissenting opinions are important and carry persuasive authority. Dissenting opinions can appeal to higher courts or the legislative branch to correct perceived judicial errors.

How do the three branches of government influence special education?

The three branches of government and the four sources of law often interact. Through a system of checks and balances, each branch of government has a means to respond to the laws of another branch. The executive branch can veto statutory laws before enactment. The legislative branch can pass new statutory laws if they disagree with regulatory laws. The judicial branch can declare statutory or regulatory laws unconstitutional. If the legislative branch does not agree with the interpretation of a law by the judicial branch, it can pass a new law.

Special education law has evolved due to this interaction between the branches of government. As will be discussed in the next chapter, Congress began passing more significant special education legislation in the 1960s and 1970s. Once that legislation was passed, the executive branch bore responsibility for carrying out the law and created regulations. Inevitably with any major piece of legislation, disputes arose about specifics within the law and how regulations were enacted. The judicial branch then got involved to settle disagreements. Being the original creators of the law, Congress was not going to let the judicial branch have the final interpretation. So, they passed new legislation based on what was learned through regulatory and case law experiences.

The interaction is not always circular. As depicted in figure 1.5, new case law may prompt the executive branch to revise regulations. Or revised

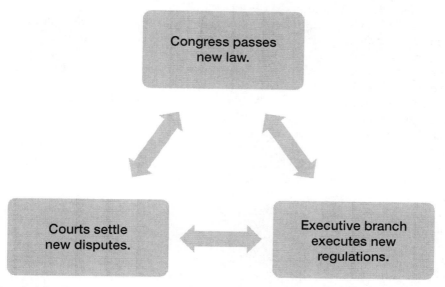

Figure 1.5 Evolution of Laws Based on the Interaction between the Branches of Government.

regulations may persuade the legislative branch to create a new law to clarify how the executive branch should regulate the law. The process of creating statutory, regulatory, and case law is long and cumbersome. It can take years for a case to work its way through the lower courts to reach a Circuit Court of Appeals or the Supreme Court. Major pieces of legislation require years to develop and pass through both chambers in Congress. Months may pass before regulations are established and trickle down to those affected on the front lines (e.g., teachers in classrooms). Yet, it is through this tedious and tiresome process that special education law has progressed to what it is today.

Where can I find more information on the three branches of government?

USA.gov (www.usa.gov). An informative website that provides in-depth information about all parts of the U.S. government. The website includes information about the three branches of government including helpful infographics. For detailed information about the three branches of government visit https://www.usa.gov/branches-of-government.

Constitution Center (constitutioncenter.org). The Constitution Center is an interactive information source about the text, history, and meaning of the U.S. Constitution. There is an interactive constitution that provides the original text as well as various interpretations from a wide range of experts. The Constitution Center also provides a media library that deals with current issues around the Constitution. For access to these resources visit https://constitutioncenter.org/interactive-constitution.

YouTube (www.youtube.com). The video streaming platform offers a wide range of informative videos. Searching "School House Rock Government Videos" provides informative videos that break down the concepts of government in a way that makes them accessible to people of all ages. For a list of videos relating to the American government visit https://www.youtube.com/watch?v=tyeJ5So3El0&list=PLZxu8fzWW7cFh8z3UlDlWCERd6chwiqCu&index=2.

Harry S. Truman Library (www.trumanlibrary.gov). The Harry S. Truman Library provides resources such as worksheets, crosswords, and games for support in learning about the branches of the U.S. government. Additionally, it provides teacher resources and answer sheets. To access these resources visit https://www.trumanlibrary.gov/education/three-branches.

Key Terms

Constituents: The people whom politicians represent from their electing district or state.

Controlling authority: Authority from higher courts over lower courts in their jurisdiction.

Court of Appeals: A court tasked with determining whether or not the law was applied correctly in the trial court.

Defendant: A person, company, or institution that is being accused of a crime.

Founders: The writers of the U.S. Constitution.

Jurisdiction: Authority granted within a defined field of responsibility.

Legal precedent: Rulings that establish legal principle and are applied to other cases with similar facts.

Parliamentary procedures: Processes by which the legislative branch drafts legislation, debates the legislation, and votes to approve or disprove the legislation.

Persuasive authority: Written opinions by lower courts or courts of other jurisdictions that a judge is not obligated to follow but which may help inform the judge's decision.

Plaintiff: A person, company, or institution that initiates a lawsuit.

Regulations: Instructions written by the executive branch that provide direction on how to implement and enforce laws passed by Congress.

Trial court: A court of law where cases are first tried with a fact-finding process and a jury to provide a verdict based on the strength of the plaintiff's or defendant's case.

Veto: A constitutional right to reject a decision or proposal made by a law-making body.

Discussion Questions

1. How do the legislative, executive, and judicial branches influence each other?

2. What is the difference between controlling authority and persuasive authority?

3. How do judges use the various sources of law to interpret the law in their courtroom?

4. Why is it important for teachers and school administrators to understand the structure of the U.S. government?

5. When a lawsuit related to special education services is brought to a trial court, what are the next steps necessary to create a change in the law?

References

Berring, R. C., & Edinger, A. E. (2005). *Finding the law* (12th ed.). Thomson/West.

Desilver, D. (2018, May 31). U.S. population keeps growing, but House of Representatives is same size as in Taft era. Retrieved from https://www.pewresearch.org/fact-tank/2018/05/31/u-s-population-keeps-growing-but-house-of-representatives-is-same-size-as-in-taft-era/

No Child Left Behind, 20 U.S.C. §16301 (2001).

United States Courts. (n.d.). Retrieved from https://www.uscourts.gov/about-federal-courts/educational-resources/about-educational-outreach/activity-resources/supreme-1

Yell, M. L. (2019). *The law and special education* (5th ed.). Pearson Education.

CHAPTER 2

The History of Special Education

> *Understanding the historical path of special education illustrates how vital it is to constantly be learning new and innovative methods for helping students learn and grow.*
>
> Leslie Majerus
> Special Education Teacher in Montana

Today we know special education is an essential right for students with disabilities, but that was not always the case. Several decades ago, special education and special educators did not even exist. The history of special education is filled with people and organizations who advocated for legal and educational protections for people with disabilities. Over the course of many years, numerous court cases, and significant legislation, special education has evolved and progressed into what it is today. Although sometimes reluctantly, the three branches of federal government have worked together to establish many of the securities students and people with disabilities rely on today. In this chapter we will discuss the history of special education and answer these essential questions:

1. Why were children with disabilities excluded from public education?
2. What is the significance of the *Brown v. Board of Education* (1954) case for children with disabilities?
3. What key court cases historically propelled special education?
4. What is the progression of federal involvement in the education of students with disabilities?
5. Where can I find more information about the history of special education?

Why were children with disabilities excluded from public education?

In the United States, public education is considered a critical element in maintaining a viable democracy (Levine & Wexler, 1981). Our founding fathers agreed that an educated **electorate** is more desirable than an uneducated electorate (Library of Congress, 2019); however, education is not mentioned in the U.S. Constitution.

As previously discussed in chapter 1, according to the Tenth Amendment, powers that are not specifically identified in the Constitution are reserved to the states. In the mid-1800s, states began passing education laws that required children to attend public schools. By 1918, every state had a **compulsory** education law for children. Yet even with these compulsory education laws, children with disabilities were often excluded from schools.

Various court rulings maintained the discrepancy between compulsory education laws and exclusion of children with disabilities. As recently as 1958, the Supreme Court of Illinois, in *Department of Public Welfare v. Hass*, ruled that Illinois' compulsory education legislation did not require the state to provide a free public education for the "feeble-minded" or "mentally deficient" because their limited intelligence did not allow them to benefit from a good education (Yell, 2019). Persuasive authority (covered in chapter 1) existed among the courts that children who were perceived to be uneducable were not guaranteed a right to public education.

Back in those days, society's understanding of disability was much more limited and ignorant than what it is today. Schools and programs did exist, however, for students who were deaf, blind, or physically impaired based on the more obvious nature of these disabilities. For example, as early as 1832, the New England Asylum for the Blind was founded. Normal cognitive abilities of these populations made it easier for courts and schools to suggest that they had the intellect to benefit from an education. Many of the thirteen disability categories recognized by the government today (to be discussed in chapter 3) such as emotional and behavioral disorders and autism were undiagnosed. Often, children with perceived neurological disabilities were simply categorized as "feeble-minded" and "idiots" (Arnett et al., 2016).

Apart from a few schools and institutions established to care for the feeble-minded, public education for children with disabilities was limited. Children with disabilities were excluded based on the precedence of ignorance and schools' unwillingness to welcome this population without the knowledge and strategies to educate them. If the courts were not going to force schools to provide students with disabilities an education, parents of children with disabilities needed to advocate, and advocate they did.

Advocacy. During the time courts were ruling schools did not have to educate children with disabilities, parents were leading the charge in advocating for their children to be included. The social climate about people with disabilities began to change as parents pressured the public and politicians. In fact, the first assistant secretary of education for Special Education and Rehabilitative

Services said, "parents had provided the energy and will to create special education programs [. . .] there would be little, if any, special education if the parents had not created it, directly or through political persuasion" (Martin, 2013, p. 22).

One professional organization that continues to have a major impact on special education is the Council for Exceptional Children (CEC). Founded in 1922 at Columbia University in New York, the CEC aimed to:

- Emphasize the education of the "special child."
- Create professional standards for special education teachers.
- Unite those interested in educating the "special child" (Kode, 2017, p. 47).

The Council for Exceptional Children continues to advocate for the educational rights of children with disabilities. With over 30,000 members, the CEC is a major force in the advocacy of special education.

What is the significance of the *Brown v. Board of Education* (1954) case for children with disabilities?

Although court cases such as the *Department of Public Welfare v. Hass* (1958) allowed schools to deny children with disabilities a public education, all that began to change with the **seminal** Supreme Court case called *Brown v. Board of Education* (1954, hereinafter *Brown*).

The *Brown* decision took place during the 1950s and 1960s civil rights movement. At that time, many people were advocating for equal opportunity and equal rights for minorities, particularly African Americans. Based on the infamous *Plessy v. Ferguson* (1896) Supreme Court decision that established the "separate but equal" precedent, states were segregating races in schools and denying black students admission to schools attended by white students. The plaintiffs (i.e., Brown) argued segregation was damaging to the educational opportunities of minorities because segregated schools were not, and could not be, equal. Thus, segregated schools violated black students' constitutional rights under the equal protection clause of the Fourteenth Amendment (covered in chapter 1). The Supreme Court unanimously ruled in favor of the plaintiff, stating that segregation based solely on an individual's unalterable characteristics (i.e., race) was unconstitutional. The *Brown* decision effectively overturned the *separate but equal* doctrine of *Plessy v. Ferguson*.

The Supreme Court reasoned in *Brown* that education in our society is of utmost importance. Negative consequences and stigmatizing effects of racial segregation harmed segregated students and denied them equal educational opportunity. Because the court ruled that segregation based on an individual's unalterable characteristics was unconstitutional, disability advocates considered the *Brown* ruling applicable to those denied an education because of disability. *Brown* was the spark for advocates to ensure educational rights for children with disabilities, because if segregation by race was a denial of equal educational opportunity, then obviously the exclusion of children with disabilities was also a denial of equal educational opportunity.

Although the *Brown* case was grounded in differential treatment between races, it was significant for special education because it established that equal opportunity applied to students with disabilities too. Societal attitudes and systemic structural change do not happen quickly. It was not until sixteen years after the *Brown* decision that two landmark federal district court cases applied the concept of equal opportunity to children with disabilities.

What key court cases historically propelled special education?

Brown may be considered the catalyst court case which established equal educational opportunity for children with disabilities under constitutional law; however, remember that *Brown* discussed equal opportunity in terms of race. Disability advocates argued that the rationale for the *Brown* decision should apply to disability as well. Two key court cases that specifically addressed excluded students with disabilities, and historically propelled special education, were *Pennsylvania Association for Retarded Children (PARC) v. Commonwealth of Pennsylvania* (1972) and *Mills v. Board of Education of the District of Colombia* (1972).

PARC v. Pennsylvania (1972). The Pennsylvania Association for Retarded Children (hereinafter *PARC*) brought a **class-action** lawsuit against Pennsylvania in a federal district court.

The plaintiffs argued that children with mental retardation were not receiving a public education. The state was disregarding its constitutional obligation to provide equal educational opportunities as supported by the equal protection clause of the Fourteenth Amendment. Four critical points emerged from the lawsuit that impacted the court's interpretation of special education:

1. Children with mental retardation are capable of benefiting from educational programs.
2. Education is not solely defined as an academic experience, thus legitimizing functional life skill outcomes (e.g., feeding, clothing, communicating) as equally important.
3. Since Pennsylvania established legislation to provide all children in Pennsylvania a free public education, the state could not deny children with mental retardation access to that free public education.
4. Early intervention for children with mental retardation increases educational outcomes. Pennsylvania could not deny preschoolers with mental retardation access to preschool programs available to preschoolers without disabilities (Zettel & Ballard, 1979).

The court ruled in favor of the plaintiffs, requiring that children with mental retardation between ages six and twenty-one receive a free public education. In addition, the court declared that educating students with mental retardation in educational programs similar to those of students without disabilities was most desirable. Persuasive authority of the *PARC* decision reverberated across the country and recognized free public education for children with mental retardation, but what about children with other disabilities?

Mills v. Board of Education (1972). Around the same time that *PARC* was in court, a separate class-action lawsuit was in the Federal District Court for the District of Columbia. *Mills v. Board of Education* (1972, hereinafter *Mills*) was filed on behalf of all children with disabilities that were excluded from public education in Washington, DC. The plaintiffs argued that based on the equal protection clause of the Fourteenth Amendment, children with disabilities were unlawfully excluded from public education without due process. The court ruled that based on the *Brown* decision (i.e., segregation by race was unconstitutional), total exclusion of children with disabilities was also unconstitutional. The court mandated Washington DC's board of education to provide all children with disabilities a free public education. Furthermore, the court required the board to provide parents of students with disabilities due process safeguards. These safeguards needed to include a right to a hearing with legal representation and an impartial hearing officer, the right to appeal, the right to have access to records, and the right to written notification of all stages of the process (Yell, 2019). The safeguard requirement of the *Mills* decision became the framework for the procedural safeguard pillar of the Individuals with Disabilities Education Act (IDEA; discussed in chapter 9).

The *PARC* and *Mills* precedents were used for similar cases to be filed across the country. Within a couple of years following *PARC* and *Mills*, forty-six additional lawsuits were filed in twenty-eight states on behalf of children with disabilities excluded from public education (Zettel & Ballard, 1979). The outcomes of those lawsuits were similar to the *PARC* and *Mills* decisions. Regardless of this progress in the courts, the adequacy of educating students with disabilities varied greatly across states. New state laws requiring the education of children with disabilities resulted in school districts and advocates complaining that insufficient funding created inadequate facilities, unavailable instructional materials, and poorly trained teachers. Eventually Congress realized the constitutional rights of children with disabilities were still being violated with inferior access to public education and that the federal government needed to act.

What is the progression of federal involvement in the education of students with disabilities?

Given that the U.S. Constitution does not mention education, there is no constitutional authority for federal government involvement in education.

However, the **spending clause** in Article 1 of the U.S. Constitution provides the federal government legal authority to offer federal grants to states that are contingent on the states doing, or stopping, certain activities. Using this spending clause authority, federal involvement in the education of children with disabilities really began in the late 1950s. The Retarded Children Act of 1958 was passed to encourage the expansion of teaching in the education of mentally retarded children with grants to institutions of higher learning and state educational agencies. Efforts and funds to develop special education, however, were limited. It was not until President Lyndon Johnson, in the 1960s, declared a "war on poverty" that the federal government significantly increased its role in public education as a whole. President Johnson believed in the ideal of education as a ladder out of poverty. His administration pushed hard for legislation that changed the trajectory of public education.

The Elementary and Secondary Education Act of 1965. The purpose of the Elementary and Secondary Education Act (ESEA) of 1965 was to grant federal money to states to improve education for **disadvantaged** children. This major piece of legislation consisted of five titles, with the largest and most impactful title being Title I. The goal of Title I was to close **academic achievement gaps** (e.g., in reading and math) between disadvantaged children and non-disadvantaged children.

Title I funds were distributed to school districts with high percentages of low-income families. In order to receive those funds, states agreed to implement requirements within the various titles and report progress back to the federal government. States could not be forced to make changes based on the ESEA; however, the incentive of extra money to support educational programming was powerful. Today, 42 percent of public schools receive Title I funds to ensure that all children meet challenging academic standards (U.S. Department of Education, 2019).

A year after the ESEA was passed, it was amended in 1966 to include Title VI to "provide grants to states to assist in the initiation, expansion, and improvement of special educational and related services for handicapped children at the preschool, elementary, and secondary school levels" (Irvin, 1968, p. 565). Title VI also created the Bureau for the Education of the Handicapped in the U.S. Office of Education, which was the first federal agency designated to coordinate federal efforts for children with disabilities.

The Education of the Handicapped Act of 1970. Only four years after Title VI was amended into the ESEA, it was removed from the ESEA and signed into law as its own piece of legislation called the Education of the Handicapped Act (EHA) of 1970. The purpose of the EHA was to consolidate and expand efforts under ESEA Title VI. Although the EHA did not include **substantive rights** for students with disabilities, it was an important piece of legislation. It was the first federal government legislation specifically and solely for students with disabilities. Moreover, the EHA mandated that students with disabilities receive the special education and related services they needed to progress (Colker, 2013).

The Education of All Handicapped Children Act of 1975. Even though Title VI and the EHA were federal laws, those pieces of legislation lacked clarity and robust implementation provisions on how states should provide public education for students with disabilities. In 1974, it was reported by Congress that 1.75 million children with disabilities were still excluded from educational opportunities, and 3 million students with disabilities were receiving an inappropriate education (Yell et al., 2004). In 1975, Congress passed, and President Ford signed, into law the most consequential piece of legislation for students with disabilities called the Education of All Handicapped Children Act (EAHCA) of 1975.

Also known as P.L. 94-142, the primary purpose of the EAHCA was to provide all children with disabilities between ages three and eighteen access to a free and appropriate public education. The compilation of court case decisions (e.g., *PARC* and *Mills*) along with advocacy efforts from parents and organizations pushed Congress into passing this sweeping legislation to codify once and for all the right to education for all children with disabilities. The EAHCA mandated many of the legal protections students with disabilities have today such as (a) nondiscriminatory evaluations, (b) education in the least restrictive environment, (c) procedural due process, (d) parental involvement in the evaluation and placement process, (e) free and appropriate education, and (f) an individualized education program (IEP).

Once legislation is passed and implementation occurs, oftentimes unintended consequences emerge or overlooked problems remain. It is common for major pieces of legislation, such as the EAHCA, to receive amendments during **reauthorization**.

In 1986, Congress amended the EAHCA to include a section of the law that offered grants to states contingent on states providing services to children with disabilities between birth and age three. Originally, the EAHCA funding was for ages between three and eighteen, yet researchers and advocates understood the importance of early intervention and thus encouraged this amendment to be adopted. The centerpiece of the Education of the Handicapped Amendments (1986) was the individualized family service plan (IFSP). An IFSP is a plan developed by a multidisciplinary and interagency team that includes the child's parents that identifies (a) the child's present levels of performance, (b) expected outcomes and goals, (c) early intervention services to meet goals, (d) the environment where early intervention services are to be delivered, (e) projected dates and duration of services, and (f) steps to support the transition of the toddler from early intervention services to special education services.

The Individuals with Disabilities Education Act of 1990. The Individuals with Disabilities Education Act (IDEA) of 1990 should be a familiar piece of legislation.

In 1990, the EAHCA was reauthorized and renamed IDEA. A few changes within the legislation occurred during reauthorization as well. The term *handicap* was replaced with *disability*. The law was updated to use "person first" language (e.g., "student with a disability" rather than "disabled student"). Moreover, two additional disability categories were added to the list of qualifying disabilities: **autism** and **traumatic brain injury**.

The new law also added a requirement that IEP teams of students who were sixteen years or older include a section within the student's IEP on transition services. Transition services were required to promote movement from school to post-school activities such as employment, continuing education (e.g., college or vocational training), and independent living. Transition planning needed to account for the student's needs, interests, and preferences. Since 1990, IDEA has undergone amendments and reauthorizations. The next chapter is devoted to essential questions about IDEA.

The No Child Left Behind Act of 2001. Remember that the pivotal legislation for special education—the EAHCA which is now IDEA—resulted from a divergence in law back when Title VI split from the ESEA (1965) as the EHA (1970). It is important to understand that the ESEA continued to be reauthorized and amended over the decades affecting *all* students attending public education, including students with disabilities. Parallel with IDEA, the ESEA progressed over the decades. Following President George W. Bush's election, he declared his number one domestic priority was to overhaul and rename the ESEA as No Child Left Behind (NCLB). This reauthorization was a significant increase in federal government involvement in public education. In fact, some claim the reauthorization of NCLB was the moment when the federal government seized responsibility for public education (Bankston, 2010). The main goal of NCLB was to close academic achievement gaps by bringing every student up to state standards in reading and math within a certain time. To continue receiving federal funds, states were required to establish progress monitoring processes to track student progress and procedures to hold schools accountable that did not make **adequate yearly progress (AYP)**.

NCLB impacted students with disabilities and special education greatly. Schools were now held accountable for all students' academic progress, and students with disabilities were a subgroup of students to be included in NCLB academic progress accountability data. Other categories included race/ethnicity, limited English proficiency, and socioeconomic status. Remember that IDEA required students with disabilities access to the general education curriculum and education among nondisabled peers. To ensure that students with disabilities were not ignored from instruction, NCLB required states to include this population in their accountability data. This marked a shift from a focus on participation for students with disabilities to academic performance. To measure progress, students with disabilities were given state assessments (alongside their nondisabled peers) for the grade standards in which they were enrolled. Anticipating discrepancies between academic ability and grade level, NCLB allowed a student's IEP team to provide state-approved accommodations during the assessments (e.g., extended time, testing in a separate location).

Students with more severe cognitive disabilities could take an alternative assessment based on achievement standards. Only 1 percent of students with disabilities, however, who passed the alternative assessment would be counted in a school's NCLB accountability data. This cap was created to prevent schools from hiding student data by disproportionately giving the alternative assessment to students who should be taking the state-administered assessment.

Another important component of NCLB was the requirement for using **scientifically based research** in all aspects of educating students with disabilities. Congress realized that fads, pseudoscience, and personal bias were causing ineffective instructional practices and academic failure. Numerous references to scientifically based research with NCLB, therefore, served as warnings to schools that untested practices with no evidence of effectiveness were intolerable (O'Neill, 2004).

TABLE 2.1   Case Law and Federal Statutory Laws That Have Shaped Special Education

Date	Case Law and Statutes	Outcome
1954	*Brown v. Board of Education*	• Segregation on the basis of race ruled unconstitutional. • Provided opportunity for disability advocates to argue that segregation on the basis of disability also unconstitutional.
1965	Elementary and Secondary Education Act (ESEA)	• First significant federal legislation aimed at improving the education for disadvantaged children through grant incentives.
1966	Title VI amendment to ESEA	• Provided federal funds for initiation, expansion, and improvement of special education.
1970	Education of the Handicapped Act (EHA)	• First stand-alone federal legislation for the education of students with disabilities.
1972	*PARC v. Commonwealth of Pennsylvania*	• Court ruled that Pennsylvania had to provide all children with mental retardation a free public education. • Legitimized functional life skills as appropriate academic outcomes. • Underscored importance of early education for children with mental retardation.
1972	*Mills v. Board of Education of the District of Colombia*	• Court ruled that because segregation by race was unconstitutional, exclusion of students with disabilities also unconstitutional. • Established framework for procedural safeguards and due process.
1975	Education of All Handicapped Children Act (EAHCA)	• Most significant piece of legislation for students with disabilities and special education. • Established the right for eligible students with disabilities between ages three and eighteen to a free appropriate education in their least restrictive environment. • Required nondiscriminatory evaluations. • Required schools to develop an individualized education program. • Required parental involvement in the evaluation and placement process. • Expanded safeguard and due process procedures.
1986	Education of the Handicapped Amendments	• Established early intervention service for children between birth and three years old. • Required IFSPs for eligible children and their families.

Date	Case Law and Statutes	Outcome
1990	Individuals with Disabilities Education Act (IDEA)	• Renamed the EAHCA as IDEA • Updated legislation with "people first" language • Replaced "handicapped" with "disability" • Added autism and traumatic brain injury as eligible categories • Added transition requirement in IEPs of students aged sixteen or older
2001	No Child Left Behind Act (NCLB)	• Renamed the ESEA as NCLB • Identified students with disabilities as a subgroup in adequate yearly progress accountability data • Required schools to use scientifically based research practices • Required all teachers to be highly qualified
2015	Every Student Succeeds Act (ESSA)	• Renamed NCLB as ESSA • Maintains high standards and accountability goals of NCLB • Less punitive than NCLB regarding adequate yearly progress • Gives states more authority and flexibility to implement accountability measures

A third component of NCLB that affected students with disabilities was that all teachers (including special education teachers) needed to meet the requirements of highly qualified. To be highly qualified, special education teachers needed to have (a) a bachelor's degree, (b) full state certification as a special education teacher or passed a state special education teacher licensing exam, and (c) passed state-administered academic standard exams in content areas taught (e.g., reading, math).

The Every Student Succeeds Act of 2015. The goals of NCLB to close achievement gaps by raising academic standards and bringing all students to 100 percent proficiency in reading and math were valid, yet unrealistic. As schools struggled to make adequate yearly progress, overly punitive measures and rigidly mandated procedures ushered in an era of "teaching to the test." In 2015, Congress reauthorized and renamed NCLB, and President Obama signed into law the Every Student Succeeds Act (ESSA). Much of ESSA maintains and builds on the goals of the ESEA and NCLB, such as ensuring educational access for all students, focusing on closing achievement gaps, promoting high standards, and holding schools accountable. Where ESSA differs from its predecessors is that it shifts authority from the federal government back to the states and local districts. States are given more authority in how they spend their funds and how they implement their accountability systems. Table 2.1 provides an overview of case laws and statutory laws that have shaped special education.

Where can I find more information about the history of special education?

Wrights Law (www.wrightslaw.com). A comprehensive website for parents, educators, advocates, and attorneys seeking accurate, reliable information about special education law, education law, and advocacy for children with disabilities. For specific information on the history of special education visit https ://www.wrightslaw.com/law/art/history.spec.ed.law.htm.

The National Association of Elementary School Principals (www.naesp.org). The National Association of Elementary School Principals (NAESP), founded in 1921, is a professional organization serving elementary and middle school principals and other education leaders throughout the United States, Canada, and overseas. For a brief PDF on the evolution of special education, visit https://www .naesp.org/sites/default/files/resources/1/Principal/2008/N-Oweb2.pdf.

Rethinking Schools (www.rethinkingschools.org). Rethinking schools is committed to equity and to the vision that public education is central to the creation of a humane, caring, multiracial democracy. While writing for a broad audience, Rethinking Schools emphasizes problems facing urban schools, particularly issues of race. For an article on the history of special education visit https://www.rethinkingschools.org/articles/the-history-of-special-education.

American Institute for Research (www.air.org). The American Institute for Research (AIR) is one of the world's largest behavioral and social science research and evaluation organizations. Their overriding goal is to use the best science available to bring the most effective ideas and approaches to enhancing everyday life. For videos and a variety of blog posts on the history of special education visit https://www.air.org/resource/individuals-disabilities-education-act-40-years-later.

The Office of Special Education and Rehabilitative Services. The Office of Special Education and Rehabilitative Services (OSERS) understands the many challenges still facing individuals with disabilities and their families. Therefore, OSERS is committed to improving results and outcomes for people with disabilities of all ages. OSERS supports programs that serve millions of children, youth, and adults with disabilities. To download a report on the progress of IDEA after 35 years in educating students with disabilities visit https://www2 .ed.gov/about/offices/list/osers/idea35/history/index.html.

Key Terms

Academic achievement gaps: Disparities in academic performance between groups of students.

Adequate yearly progress (AYP): The amount of yearly improvement each Title I school and district are expected to make in order to enable low-achieving children to meet high performance levels expected of all children.

Autism: A developmental disability significantly affecting verbal and nonverbal communication and social interaction, usually evident before age three, and which adversely affects a child's educational performance.

Class-action: A type of lawsuit where one of the parties is a group of people who are represented collectively by a member of that group.

Compulsory: Required by law; obligatory.

Disadvantaged: Students from impoverished families.

Electorate: People in a country who are entitled to vote.

Reauthorization: A renewal of the authority, legal power, or right of.

Scientifically based research: Systematic and empirical research that (a) uses observation or experiments with rigorous data analyses to test the stated hypotheses, (b) relies on measurements or observational methods that provide valid data across evaluators and observers, and (c) has been accepted by a peer-reviewed journal or approved by a panel of independent experts through a comparatively rigorous, objective, and scientific review.

Seminal: Strongly influencing later developments.

Spending clause: "The Congress shall have power to lay and collect taxes, duties, imposts and excises, to pay the debts and provide for the common defense and general welfare of the United States [. . .]" Article 1, Section 8, Clause 1.

Substantive rights: Protections of the content and quality of educational services.

Traumatic brain injury: An acquired injury to the brain caused by an external physical force, resulting in total or partial functional disability or psychosocial impairment, or both, that adversely affects a child's educational performance.

Discussion Questions

1. Why did the federal government get involved in the education of students with disabilities?

2. How does *Brown v. Board of Education* (1954) relate to students with disabilities?

3. Why do we need to identify students with disabilities?

4. What would happen if the U.S. Constitution were amended to include a provision about the right to an education? Should it be amended?

5. What does the future of special education look like?

References

Arnett, S., Fitzpatrick, M., & Theoharis, N. R. (2016). *Foundation of special education: Understanding students with exceptionalities.* Kendall Hunt Publishing.

Bankston, I. C. L. (2010). Federal control of public schools and the decline of community. *Modern Age, 52*(3), 184-197. Retrieved from http://search.ebscohost.com.mutex.gmu.edu/login.aspx?direct=true&db=ehh&AN=57631409&site=ehost-live

Colker, R. (2013). *Disabled education: A critical analysis of the Individuals with Disabilities Education Act*. NYU Press.

Dept. of Public Welfare v. Haas, 154 N.E.2d 265 (Ill. 1958).

Irvin, T. B. (1968). Assistance to states for education of handicapped children under ESEA title VI-A. *Exceptional Children, 34*(7), 565-568.

Kode, K. (2017). *Elizabeth Farrell and the history of special education*. The Council for Exceptional Children.

Levine, E. L., & Wexler, E. M. (1981). *P.L. 94-142: An act of Congress*. Macmillan.

Library of Congress. (2019). *Thomas Jefferson*. Retrieved from https://www.loc.gov/exhibits/jefferson/60.html

Martin, E. W. (2013). *Breakthrough: Special education legislation 1965-1981*. Bardolf & Company.

O'Neill, P. T. (2004). *No Child Left Behind compliance manual*. Brownstone Publications.

U.S. Department of Education. (2019). Title I part A. Retrieved January 11, 2019, from https://www2.ed.gov/programs/titleiparta/index.html

Yell, M. L. (2019). *The law and special education* (5th ed.). Pearson Education.

Yell, M. L., Drasgow, E., Bradley, R., & Justesen, T. (2004). Critical legal issues in special education. In A. McCray Sorrells, H. J. Reith, & P. T. Sindelar (Eds.), *Issues in special education* (pp. 16-37). Allyn & Bacon.

Zettel, J. J., & Ballard, J. (1979). The Education for All Handicapped Children Act of 1975 PL 94-142: Its history, origins, and concepts. *Journal of Education, 161*(3), 5-22.

CHAPTER 3

Individuals with Disabilities Education Act

> IDEA is the key that opened the door for students with disabilities in 1975, allowing students and their families to have procedural safeguards and an equal education.
>
> Nancy J. Holsapple, PhD
> Indiana Director of Special Education

The result of decades of advocacy, litigation, and legislation is the Individuals with Disabilities Education Act (IDEA) of 2004. This federal statute is currently the guiding document for special education programs and services. When first passed in 1975 as the Education of All Handicapped Children Act (EAHCA), Congress promised to provide 40 percent of excess funding costs to assist states in educating students with disabilities. In reality, the federal government has only covered around 15 percent of the additional cost for educating students with disabilities (Congressional Research Service, 2019). Regardless of funding shortfalls, all fifty states are required to follow IDEA laws and regulations. In addition, all fifty states have passed state legislation that mirrors IDEA yet provides greater details and specifics regarding individual state special education services. Even though there are opportunities for improvement, IDEA should be championed as it has successfully provided educational services to millions of students with disabilities (U.S. Department of Education, 2010). In this chapter we will discuss IDEA and answer these essential questions:

1. What is the purpose of the Individuals with Disabilities Education Act?
2. What is the structure of the Individual with Disabilities Education Act?

3. How does the Individuals with Disabilities Education Act, Section 504, and the Americans with Disabilities Act (ADA) interrelate?
4. Where can I find more information about the Individuals with Disabilities Education Act, Section 504, and the ADA?

What is the purpose of the Individuals with Disabilities Education Act?

Disability is a natural part of the human experience and in no way diminishes the right of individuals to participate in or contribute to society. Improving educational results for children with disabilities is an essential element of our national policy of ensuring equality of opportunity, full participation, independent living, and economic self-sufficiency for individuals with disabilities. (Education of All Handicapped Children Act of 1975)

Prior to the enactment of the Education of All Handicapped Children Act of 1975 (hereinafter referred to as IDEA), children with disabilities were often excluded from public education. States and local school districts did not have adequate training and resources to meet the needs of children with disabilities. Moreover, children with disabilities were often not even diagnosed. When Congress decided to act, pass legislation, and permanently alter the narrative about disability, they wrote that the purpose of IDEA was to

ensure that all children with disabilities have available to them a free appropriate public education that emphasizes special education and related services designed to meet their unique needs and prepare them for further education, employment, and independent living; to ensure that the rights of children with disabilities and parents of such children are protected; to assist states, localities, educational service agencies, and Federal agencies to provide for the education of all children with disabilities. (IDEA, 2004)

Children with disabilities are only protected under IDEA if they meet IDEA's definition of a student with a disability. IDEA uses a categorical approach to define students with disabilities. Figure 3.1 is a list of thirteen disability categories that students can qualify under as determined on an individual basis by a student's **multidisciplinary team**. Over the years, terminologies have changed. For example, in 2010, President Obama signed a law requiring the federal government to replace the categorical term "mental retardation" with "intellectual disability."

It is important to note that not all students with disabilities automatically qualify for protections under IDEA. Because IDEA is about providing educational service, only students whose disabilities adversely impact their education are eligible for special education. A student may have a diagnosed hearing impairment; however, if that hearing impairment does not negatively affect their educational progress, they would not qualify for special education, and would likely receive a Section 504 plan.

**Categories of Disabilities
Under IDEA**

- Autism
- Deaf-blindness
- Deafness
- Hearing Impairment
- Intellectual disability
- Multiple disabilities
- Orthopedic impairments
- Other health impairments
- Emotional disturbance
- Specific learning disability
- Speech or language impairment
- Traumatic brain injury
- Visual impairment or blindness

Figure 3.1 Categories of Disabilities under IDEA.

What is the structure of the Individuals with Disabilities Education Act?

Based on the comprehensiveness of the law, IDEA is an extensive 162-page legal document. It is separated into four parts (A, B, C, and D). Table 3.1 is a general overview of each part of IDEA.

Part A. Any statute will have a general provisions section. Within Part A is where Congress explains the purpose and goals of the law. Relevant facts regarding the education of students with disabilities are also presented in Part A. It is important to provide definitions of key terms within any statute so that there is agreement among all **stakeholders.**

These definitions are intended to assist stakeholders in a standard implementation, though more subjective terms nevertheless tend to spark litigation, such as the definition of "appropriate" as we will read about in chapter 4.

Part B. Most special education teachers and administrators should be familiar with Part B of IDEA. This part addresses the education of students with disabilities between the ages of three and twenty-one. Part B is by far the largest section of IDEA as it accounts for nearly 95 percent of all IDEA **expenditures** (Congressional Research Service, 2019).

To receive Part B funding, states submit special education plans meeting IDEA's requirements. **Provisions** within Part B demand states to ensure all students who qualify for special education are protected under six key principles.

These principles are (a) a free and appropriate public education (FAPE), (b) the guarantee of a nondiscriminatory evaluation, (c) education in the student's

TABLE 3.1 The Four Parts of IDEA

Section	Title	Description
Part A	General provisions	Outlines IDEA's general provisions, including the purpose of IDEA and the definitions used throughout the statute.
Part B	Assistance for education of all children with disabilities	Includes provisions related to formula grants that assist states in providing a free appropriate public education in the least restrictive environment for children with disabilities ages three through twenty-one.
Part C	Infants and toddlers with disabilities	Includes provisions related to formula grants that assist states in providing early intervention services for infants and toddlers birth through age two and their families.
Part D	National activities to improve education of children with disabilities	Includes provisions related to discretionary grants to support state personnel development, technical assistance and dissemination, technology, and parent-training and information centers.

least restrictive environment (LRE), (d) an individualized education program (IEP), (e) the right for parent participation in their child's education, and (f) procedural safeguards to protect the interests of students and their families. Each principle is often called a **pillar of special education** (figure 3.2). Subsequent chapters will discuss each pillar in greater detail.

Part C. The importance of early intervention for young children with disabilities is well established in research (National Early Childhood Technical Assistance Center, 2011). Part C of IDEA is crafted to support families and their infants (birth through age two) with disabilities, or at risk for substantial developmental disabilities. It provides grants to states who implement statewide **interagency programs** of early intervention services. Services may include training for families, counseling, occupational and physical therapy, speech pathology, medical services, or other services depending on the individual needs of a family and their child.

Unlike Part B of IDEA where students receive an IEP, eligible children under Part C receive an individualized family service plan (IFSP).

The IFSP is developed among appropriate stakeholders, including the child's family members. It is a guiding document describing the concerns of the family, the child's present levels of function and need, services the child and family will receive, where services will take place, and for how long. A key principle of an

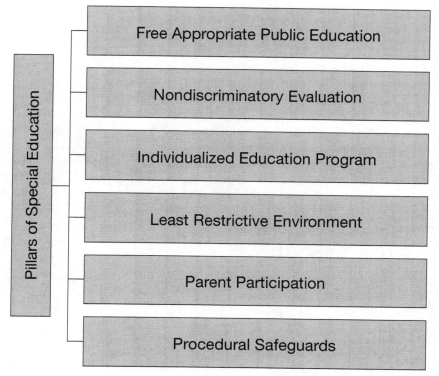

Figure 3.2 Six Pillars of Special Education.

IFSP is that services are provided in a natural environment, a place where the family and child are comfortable (usually at home).

Part D. With competitive grants, Part D aims at enhancing the education of children with disabilities on a national level. State Educational Agencies (SEAs) are offered competitive grants to help improve their systems, prepare their special education personnel, and improve education for children with disabilities in general. Universities and non-profit organizations are other entities that are eligible for competitive grants. Universities typically seek Part D funding for recruitment and development of special education programs, teachers, and faculty. Grants can support non-profit organizations in developing information centers and educating parents on various issues, including the importance of early intervention and special education. Less than 2 percent of IDEA funding is directed toward projects under Part D (Congressional Research Service, 2019).

How do the Individuals with Disabilities Education Act, Section 504, and the Americans with Disabilities Act interrelate?

The Individuals with Disabilities Education Act is not the only federal legislation that protects people with disabilities. Antidiscrimination advocacy ultimately led the federal government to pass two other significant pieces of legislation that require exploration.

Section 504. The Rehabilitation Act of 1973 was the first major legislative attempt to prohibit discrimination on the basis of disability. There are several sections to the act, but in terms of education and schools Section 504 of the Rehabilitation Act is the most relevant. Simply called Section 504, this part of the law prohibits discrimination against qualified individuals with disabilities by any program or activity receiving federal financial assistance. Given that nearly all public schools receive federal money, Section 504 applies to public K–12 schools as well as universities that receive federal assistance or have students that receive federal financial assistance (e.g., student loans). Section 504 is not an education-based law; rather, it is a civil rights law, meaning that it protects not only students with disabilities, but parents with disabilities as well as employees from discrimination. Discrimination in schools occurs when someone with a disability is excluded from participation or receives different treatment because of their disability (Yell, 2019). The statute specifically states:

> No other qualified individual with a disability in the United States shall, solely by reason of his or her disability, be excluded from the participation in, be denied the benefits of, or be subjected to discrimination under any program or any activity receiving federal financial assistance. (Rehabilitation Act of 1973)

To qualify for protections under Section 504, the statute defines "disability" as

> Any person who (a) has a physical or mental impairment which substantially limits one or more of such person's major life activities, (b) has a record of such an impairment, or (c) is regarded as having such an impairment.

Physical impairment	Mental impairment	Major life activity
Any physiological disorder or condition, cosmetic disfigurement, or anatomical loss affecting a major body system (e.g., neurological, cardiovascular, respiratory, etc.)	Any mental or psychological disorder, such as intellectual disability, emotional or mental disability, organic brain syndrome, etc.	Functions such as caring for one's self, performing manual tasks, walking, seeing, hearing, breathing, learning and working

Figure 3.3 Section 504 and ADA Definitions of Physical Impairment, Mental Impairment, and Major Life Activity.

Figure 3.3 provides further detail on the qualifications for disability under Section 504 (and the Americans with Disabilities Act [ADA]).

In regard to education, Section 504 has four major principles. The first principle is protection from discrimination. This principle ensures people with disabilities have an equal opportunity, such as their nondisabled peers, to benefit from academic or nonacademic school programs. Often referred to as the comparability requirement (Ferreri, 2019), schools are required to provide comparable opportunity for benefit. To do so, schools need to provide **reasonable accommodations** for physical or programmatic access. "Reasonable accommodation" is a subjective term, although courts have provided some guidance on what is not reasonable, such as excessive financial and administrative burdens based on the size, type, and budget of the program.

The second principle is evaluation and placement. In terms of discrimination, a person does not have to have a documented disability to be discriminated against under Section 504.

They could be "regarded as having" a disability, and therefore discriminated against. For example, a student may be perceived as having an emotional disability and not allowed to attend a field trip. The student is being treated differently due to a perceived "mental impairment." This could be an act of discrimination under Section 504. When it comes to providing reasonable accommodations, however, the person with a disability must have a documented physical or mental disability that limits a major life activity. It is the responsibility of the individual (or parent, if it is a student) to provide the school with proof of the disability.

Once a school receives notice of a documented disability under Section 504, the school is responsible for providing the third principle, a free appropriate public education (FAPE). Among a team of stakeholders (e.g., teacher, parent, 504 school coordinator), a 504 plan is developed to document the reasonable accommodations or **related services** that a student will receive to meet their needs in their least restrictive environment (LRE) as adequately as the needs of their nondisabled peers. The definition of "appropriate" in FAPE for Section 504 differs from the definition in IDEA (as we shall see in chapter 4). In Section 504 it is a term of equivalency. If a student is granted free access to a **comparable public education**, as their nondisabled peers, the requirement of FAPE is met.

The fourth principle of Section 504 is procedural safeguards. Schools must have due process procedures in place for parents or guardians to follow if a disagreement arises. Procedural safeguards offer parents and guardians numerous rights, such as the right to file a grievance with the school district, the right to review their child's records, the right to an impartial hearing, and more.

IDEA versus Section 504. It is important to understand some similarities and differences between IDEA and Section 504. First, if a student qualifies for special education under IDEA, they are automatically covered for antidiscrimination protection under Section 504. IDEA affords protection only for children and students (birth through age twenty-one) who qualify under one or more of the thirteen disability categories, and where the disability affects educational progress. Section 504 applies to all persons with disabilities that affect a major life activity. In general, IDEA is a more robust and comprehensive piece of legislation compared to Section 504. IDEA requires a more complete evaluation process, a more detailed individualized plan, more thorough progress monitoring, and a more complex due process procedure. Figure 3.4 highlights an important court case about due process procedures between IDEA and Section 504.

Americans with Disabilities Act. Even though Section 504 established antidiscrimination legislation, the scope only reached to programs receiving federal financial assistance. Congress realized that discrimination against people with disabilities continued to exist in housing, transportation, employment, recreation, health services, voting, and much more (Yell, 2019). Therefore, in 1990, Congress extended the civil rights and antidiscrimination protections under Section 504 to essentially all aspects of public life. Congress passed, and President George H. W. Bush signed into law, the ADA. The purpose of the law was clear and boldly stated:

1. To provide a clear and comprehensive national mandate for the elimination of discrimination against individuals with disabilities.
2. To provide clear, strong, consistent, enforceable standards addressing discrimination against individuals with disabilities.
3. To ensure that the federal government plays a central role in enforcing the standards established in the Act on behalf of individuals with disabilities.
4. To invoke the sweep of Congressional authority, including the power to enforce the Fourteenth Amendment and to regulate commerce, in order to address the major areas of discrimination faced day to day by people with disabilities. (Americans with Disabilities Act of 1990)

Fry v. Napoleon Community Schools (2017)

Facts of the case

Ehlena Fry was born with cerebral palsy which impaired her motor skills and mobility. In 2008, Fry's pediatrician prescribed a service dog named Wonder. Wonder was to help Ehlena with mobility issues such as opening doors, picking up dropped items, and helping her balance as she transferred from her chair to the toilet. Ehlena's elementary school (a school within Napoleon Community Schools) denied Ehlena permission to bring her service dog to school. The school argued that a human aide could provide all the necessary help so that Ehlena could get a free and appropriate public education. Eventually the school allowed Wonder to accompany Ehlena in school for a trial period. However, Wonder had to sit in the back of the classroom and was not allowed to be with Ehlena during lunch time, recess, in the library or computer labs, and other school activities. After the trial period, the school again denied Ehlena the ability to have a service dog in school.

The Fry family sued the Napoleon Community Schools under Section 504 of the Rehabilitation Act and the American with Disabilities Act (ADA) for among other things, the denial of equal access. The Napoleon Community Schools moved to dismiss the lawsuit claiming that the Frys needed to follow due process under the Individuals with Disabilities Education Act (IDEA).

Legal issue at stake

Before the courts was an issue of whether families protected under IDEA had to follow IDEA due process procedures or could they file lawsuits under Section 504 due process procedures. The circuit courts agreed with the Napoleon Community Schools that because the lawsuit implicated IDEA, and that including Wonder in Ehlena's education served as an educational goal, then IDEA due process must be followed.

The Supreme Court ruling

The Supreme Court ruled unanimously in favor of the Fry family stating that the denial of Wonder represented disability-based discrimination and was not a denial of a free and appropriate public education (FAPE) under IDEA. Therefore, the Frys did not have to exhaust due process procedures under IDEA. The Supreme Court posed two questions that could be used by courts for future disputes between Section 504 and IDEA due process claims:

Could the family have brought essentially the same claim if the alleged conduct had occurred at a public facility such as a library or public theater?

Could an adult at the school, such as an employee or visitor, have raised the same complaint?

Figure 3.4 Important Court Case.

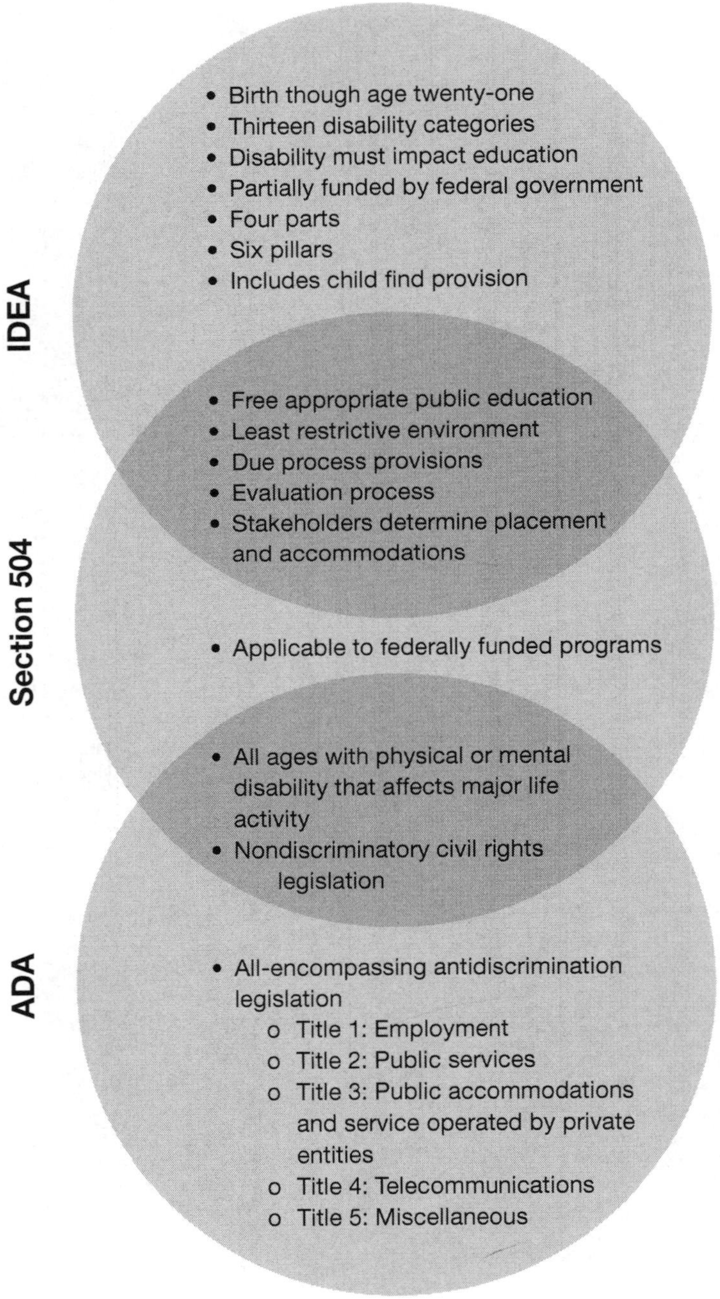

IDEA
- Birth though age twenty-one
- Thirteen disability categories
- Disability must impact education
- Partially funded by federal government
- Four parts
- Six pillars
- Includes child find provision

- Free appropriate public education
- Least restrictive environment
- Due process provisions
- Evaluation process
- Stakeholders determine placement and accommodations

Section 504
- Applicable to federally funded programs

- All ages with physical or mental disability that affects major life activity
- Nondiscriminatory civil rights legislation

ADA
- All-encompassing antidiscrimination legislation
  o Title 1: Employment
  o Title 2: Public services
  o Title 3: Public accommodations and service operated by private entities
  o Title 4: Telecommunications
  o Title 5: Miscellaneous

Figure 3.5 Similarities and Differences between IDEA (2004), Section 504 (1973), and ADA (1990).

Section 504 versus ADA. The definition of "disability" under the ADA is identical to Section 504 (see figure 3.3). The major difference between the two laws is the scope in which people with disabilities are protected. The scope of protection under the ADA was greatly expanded to include nearly all aspects of public life. Protection of individuals with disabilities under the ADA is separated across five titles: Title I employment, Title II public services, Title III public accommodations and services operated by private entities, Title IV telecommunications, and Title V miscellaneous provisions. Figure 3.5 highlights the similarities and differences between IDEA, Section 504, and the ADA.

Where can I find more information about the Individuals with Disabilities Education Act, Section 504, and the Americans with Disabilities Act?

Franklin County Law Library. A database that provides links to each individual state's special education laws and regulations. To access your state visit http://fclawlib.libguides.com/specialeducation/50statesurvey.

Parent and Educator Resource Guide to Section 504 in Public Elementary and Secondary Schools. A lengthy and comprehensive guide for how to navigate the laws and regulations of Section 504 that provides easy-to-understand definitions and descriptions. To access this document visit https://www2.ed.gov/about/offices/list/ocr/docs/504-resource-guide-201612.pdf.

ADA National Network. A great resource that provides more information about each title of the ADA, videos, fact sheets, handbooks, and guides. Additional information is also provided on the American Disability Act. To access this information visit https://adata.org/learn-about-ada.

Center for Parent Information and Resources (parentcenterhub.org). Resources that provide information on the Individuals with Disabilities Education Act (IDEA) that are available in English and Spanish. Resources including summaries, guidance, and training materials for IDEA can be accessed here: https://www.parentcenterhub.org/idea/.

U.S. Department of Education—Office of Special Education and Rehabilitative Services. Individuals with Disabilities Education Act—40 years later. A link to a brief video about IDEA and stories of how IDEA has made a difference in the lives of individuals with disabilities: https://www2.ed.gov/about/offices/list/osers/idea40/index.html.

Key Terms

Comparable public education: An education of equivalence to nondisabled peers. Does not have to be an exact replication of education but must be comparable.

Expenditures: The amount of money spent.

Interagency programs: Programs that bring together professionals from various disciplines such as occupational therapy, speech pathology, medical services, and counseling.

Multidisciplinary team: A group of individuals from multiple disciplines (e.g., special education teacher, general education teacher, psychologist, principal) who evaluate a student for special education and collaborate to create an individualized education program.

Pillar of special education: Major principle of IDEA that focuses on students' rights and the responsibilities of public schools to students with disabilities.

Provisions: A required directive within a law to protect the interests of one or both parties in a contract.

Reasonable accommodations: Accommodations that provide opportunities for students with disabilities in comparison to their nondisabled peers without excessive financial or administrative burdens.

Related services: Transportation and such developmental, corrective, and other supportive services as are required to help a child with a disability benefit from special education.

Stakeholders: Persons with an interest in something regarding a particular outcome.

Discussion Questions

1. How has IDEA changed public education in the United States?
2. What would change if the original congressional promise of 40 percent federal funding for IDEA became a reality?
3. Why are Section 504 and the ADA so important for people with disabilities?
4. How can future congressional leaders improve IDEA?
5. How can future congressional leaders improve Section 504 and the ADA?

References

American with Disabilities Act of 1990, 42 U.S.C. § 12101.

Congressional Research Service. (2019). *The Individuals with Disabilities Education Act (IDEA) funding: A primer.* Retrieved from https://fas.org/sgp/crs/misc/R44624.pdf

Education of All Handicapped Children Act of 1975, 20 U.S.C. § 1401.

Ferreri, F. (2019). *What do I do when . . .? The answer book on Section 504.* LRP Publications.

Individuals with Disabilities Education Act of 2004, 20 U.S.C. § 1400.

National Early Childhood Technical Assistance Center. (2011). *The importance of early intervention for infants and toddlers with disabilities and their families.* Retrieved from https://ectacenter.org/~pdfs/pubs/importanceofearlyintervention.pdf

Rehabilitation Act of 1973, Section 504 Regulations, 34 C.F.R § 104.1.

U.S. Department of Education. (2010). *Thirty-five years of progress in educating children with disabilities through IDEA.* Washington, DC Retrieved from https://files.eric.ed.gov/fulltext/ED515893.pdf

Yell, M. L. (2019). *The law and special education* (5th ed.). Pearson Education.

PART II

Pillars of IDEA

CHAPTER 4

Free Appropriate
Public Education

> *A free appropriate public education is a federal right granted to students with disabilities to ensure equitable access to the general education curriculum.*
>
> Donna Bort
> *Special Education Teacher in Ohio*

Prior to passing the Education for All Handicapped Children Act in 1975 (EAHCA), Congress estimated that millions of children with disabilities were excluded from public schools. In addition, millions of students with disabilities that were attending public schools were not receiving an education that was appropriate for their needs (Yell & Bateman, 2017). Through the EAHCA, Congress offered federal financial assistance to states to help them develop and improve educational programs for students with disabilities. In order to receive this financial assistance, states needed to submit plans to the federal government, detailing how students with disabilities were provided the right to a free appropriate public education (FAPE).

We know the EAHCA (1975) was reauthorized several times over the decades and is now the Individuals with Disabilities Education Act (IDEA) of 2004. Although changes to the legislation have occurred (e.g., the addition of disabilities categories), FAPE remains one of the six critical pillars of special education that were first established in 1975. It is also a pillar of special education that has generated substantial debate and litigation that continues today. In this chapter we will discuss the first pillar of special education, FAPE (figure 4.1), and answer these essential questions:

1. What is free appropriate public education?
2. What regulations and court cases have defined free appropriate public education?

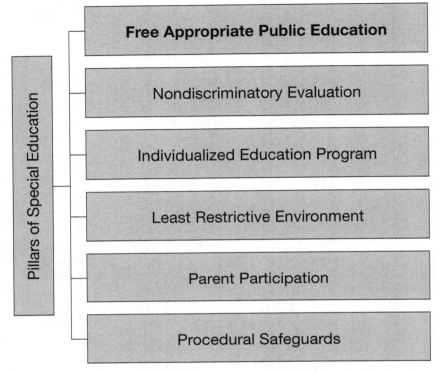

Figure 4.1 Free Appropriate Public Education Is the First Pillar of Special Education.

3. How do I ensure free appropriate public education?
4. Where can I find more information about free appropriate public education?

What is free appropriate public education?

Students who qualify as having a disability under IDEA in one or more of the thirteen categories are eligible to receive special education and **related services** (see chapter 11 for more information on related services).

The legislative authors of IDEA understood that special education and related services would be different for each child depending on that child's unique educational needs. Therefore, a FAPE definition could not be written into the law; rather, FAPE needed to be determined on a case-by-case basis. Specific services for one student may not be appropriate for another student. It all depends on a student's individual needs. To best understand the concept of FAPE, we will explore each component, starting with the more **objective** terms, *free* and *public*. Then we will explore the more **subjective** term, *appropriate*.

Free education. Free education simply means that schools may not charge parents or guardians of students with disabilities for any special education or related service. All services must be provided by schools at no expense to the family of an eligible student. IDEA does allow fees to be charged to parents of students with disabilities to the same extent that fees are charged to parents of students without disabilities, for example, field trips, art supplies, and technology fees.

A second important aspect of free education is that schools may not refuse to provide any special education or related service due to the cost of those services. When individual education program (IEP) teams plan a student's special education services, they cannot consider the cost when determining if that service is appropriate. For example, if a student's evaluation determines that the student requires physical therapy services, the IEP team must provide physical therapy services, regardless of cost. The only time an IEP team can consider cost of service is when there are two or more services that are appropriate for the student's educational need. Let's say a student with severe medical needs requires a residential placement. If there are two residential facilities that both provide appropriate services, only then can the IEP team consider cost between the programs when making a placement decision.

Public education. All students who qualify for special education under IDEA are entitled to a preschool, elementary, and secondary education that meets state standards. Given that states are responsible for education (per the Tenth Amendment), states have the freedom to set educational standards, although some requirements are established in IDEA such as when **transition planning** should take place (see chapter 11 for more information on transition services). Namely, IDEA requires IEP teams to begin transition planning when a student is 16 years old. States, therefore, must meet this minimum requirement to receive IDEA funding. States can set more demanding standards, for example, requiring transition planning at the age of fourteen (e.g., Indiana). However, states cannot set standards less demanding than those of the federal government.

All children with disabilities are entitled to a free and public education. Yet sometimes parents choose to place their child in a private school (e.g., for religious purposes) even though a free public school is available. If the parents do so, the child's right to a FAPE has been waived and the school district is not responsible for providing special education services or paying the private school tuition. The school district is not required to provide FAPE in a private school, as long as the school district has a free and appropriate education available in a public school. If a school district, however, cannot provide a student with appropriate special education services in a public school, then the school district is responsible for covering the costs of a private school tuition in order to provide a free and appropriate education. Although the concepts of "free" and "public education" are straightforward, the difficulty over the years for schools and courts has been determining what an "appropriate" education is.

Appropriate education. There is no clear-cut definition of appropriate education because the meaning of the word "appropriate" depends on circumstances. The circumstances of one student with a disability can vary greatly compared to the circumstances of another student with a disability. This means that the appropriateness of special education services depends on each individual child. Congress realized that special education services need to be **individualized** and required all students who qualify under IDEA to have an IEP.

It is the responsibility of the school to develop the IEP in cooperation with the student's parents or guardians. The written document describes the student's educational needs and details the services that will be provided. We will explore essential questions about IEPs in chapter 6, yet it is important to remember that a student's IEP is the primary evidence of an appropriate education (Bateman, 2017). An IEP documents a student's individual circumstances and the special education services that are provided to meet those circumstances. The IEP, therefore, is the core of a student's FAPE (Bateman, 2017).

What regulations and court cases have defined free appropriate public education?

The definition of FAPE has not changed within IDEA since it was first passed in 1975. IDEA (2004) states that the term "free appropriate public education" means special education and related services that:

a. Have been provided at public expense, under public supervision and direction, and without charge.
b. Meet the standards of the state educational agency.
c. Include an appropriate preschool, elementary school, or secondary school education in the state involved.
d. Are provided in conformity with the individualized education program.

Given the subjectivity of the word "appropriate," determining what constitutes an appropriate education has led to frequent disagreements between parents and schools. Shortly after schools were required to provide FAPE in 1975, court cases rose from local and state levels into the federal court system. In the early 1980s, U.S. Circuit Courts of Appeals were hearing cases to provide guidance and definitions on appropriate education. Eventually, the U.S. Supreme Court decided to consider the meaning of FAPE in 1982 to provide guidance for all lower courts and set a national standard. The *Board of Education of the Hendrick Hudson School District v. Rowley* (1982) was the first special education case heard by the U.S. Supreme Court.

Board of Education of the Hendrick Hudson School District v. Rowley (1982). Amy Rowley qualified for special education as a student who was deaf under IDEA in the Hendrick Hudson School District in New York. Prior to entering kindergarten, her IEP team decided to place Amy in a general education kindergarten class, and the principal agreed to provide Amy with a sign language interpreter. When Amy started kindergarten, however, there was no sign language interpreter. School district officials told the principal to exhaust all other options before assigning a sign language interpreter (Smith, 1996). Understandably, Amy's parents (who were also deaf) were upset. Eventually, the principal agreed to place a sign language interpreter in Amy's class for a four-week trial period. After only two weeks, though, the interpreter was removed because Amy had a negative reaction to him. Amy went on to successfully complete her kindergarten year without an interpreter.

Prior to entering first grade, Amy's IEP was developed which placed her in a general education classroom. She was to continue using her hearing aid, along with receiving tutoring and speech services. A sign language interpreter was, again, not provided. Her parents filed a **due process hearing** claiming that the school's refusal to provide a sign language interpreter had denied Amy a FAPE.

The state courts agreed with the school district that an interpreter was not needed for Amy to receive a FAPE. However, after Amy's parents sued in federal court, the federal district court claimed the school district had denied Amy a FAPE by refusing to provide an interpreter. The school district then appealed the decision to the U.S. Court of Appeals for the Second Circuit and lost. The Court of Appeals agreed with the federal district court that the school had denied Amy an "opportunity to achieve [her] full potential commensurate with the opportunity provided to the other children" (*Board of Education of the Hendrick Hudson School District v. Rowley*, 1982, p. 534). The school district then appealed the decision to the U.S. Supreme Court.

The Supreme Court recognized that uncertainty around the meaning of FAPE had caused conflicting lower court rulings. The Supreme Court, therefore, agreed to hear the *Rowley* case to answer two questions: what is a FAPE? and what is the role of state and federal courts in reviewing special education decisions? In a six–three decision, the Supreme Court ruled in favor of the school district that an interpreter was not needed for Amy to receive "educational benefit" from special education services. The Supreme Court noted that the purpose of FAPE was to provide students with disabilities a "basic floor of opportunity," not to maximize a child's educational potential. Since Amy was doing well in school and was academically above her peers, the Supreme Court stated the school district had provided Amy with an appropriate education, and the district did not need to maximize her education.

The Rowley standard. To assist lower courts in determining the appropriateness of special education services in future disputes, the Supreme Court developed the Rowley standard. The Rowley standard is a two-part test that courts can ask to determine if FAPE has been provided. The two-part test asks:

1. Has the school complied with the procedures of IDEA?
2. Is the IEP developed through IDEA's procedures reasonably calculated to enable the child to receive educational benefits?

The first part of the test established **procedural rights** for students with disabilities and their families. A court could determine that a school district had denied a student FAPE if the district did not follow required procedures (Yell, 2019). For example, school districts must complete requested evaluations within a certain time frame (e.g., sixty days); parents must be invited to join and included on their child's IEP team; and an IEP meeting must take place within ten school days if a student's change in educational placement occurs. These are examples of specific procedures that schools must follow as outlined in IDEA. If a court determines that the procedures of IDEA have been violated and they prevented the student from receiving an education, then FAPE has been denied.

The second part of the test established **substantive rights** for students with disabilities and their families. This part of the test required courts to examine the substance of a student's IEP to determine whether the IEP was reasonably calculated to enable the student to receive educational benefit (Yell, 2019). Examples of an IEP's substance include parts such as the student's present levels of academic and functional performance, annual goals and objectives, progress monitoring, related services, transition services (if age appropriate), and others. The substantive part of the Rowley standard has been a more difficult question for courts to rule on than the procedural part (Yell et al., 2016). Disagreements between courts have arisen when trying to determine what constitutes educational benefit for an individual student.

Higher and lower educational benefit standards. Following the Rowley standard directive from the Supreme Court, parents of children with disabilities continued to challenge school districts to provide the best special education services possible. As these cases were appealed and rose up the judicial jurisdiction ladder, a split among the U.S. Circuit Courts of Appeals emerged. The Third and Sixth Circuit Courts of Appeals adopted a higher educational benefit standard. These circuit courts interpreted the Rowley standard to require that an IEP must confer *meaningful* educational benefit and that trivial benefit was not sufficient to provide FAPE (Yell & Bateman, 2017).

The Second, Fourth, Seventh, Eighth, Tenth, and Eleventh Circuit Courts of Appeals adopted a lower educational benefit standard that required school districts to provide services that confer educational benefit slightly more than trivial or de minimis.

Arguments for a lower, or de minimis, standard of Rowley were often accompanied with the Chevrolet versus Cadillac analogy. The analogy suggests that because the Supreme Court interpreted IDEA to only require a basic floor of opportunity, school districts are not obligated to provide a Cadillac program of services to maximize a student's educational potential. Rather, a serviceable Chevrolet is sufficient to ensure a student receives some educational benefit. This analogy has often been used by school districts and judges to advocate for a lower educational benefit standard (see: *Doe ex rel. Doe v. Bd. of Ed. of Tullahoma City Sch.*, 1993).

Given the split in interpretation of educational benefit by the U.S. Circuit Courts of Appeals, the Supreme Court decided to step in to settle the dispute. The question the Supreme Court needed to answer was: what is the **level of educational benefit** school districts must confer on students with disabilities to provide them with FAPE?

Endrew F. v. Douglas County School District (2017). Endrew, known as Drew by his parents and teachers, was a fourth-grade student receiving special education services as a student with autism and attention deficit hyperactivity disorder. Drew had attended the Douglas County School District since he was in preschool. Over the years, though, Drew's parents became dissatisfied with his special education services. Drew's parents believed his behavior was worsening and that his academic progress had stalled. They noticed that his IEP goals did not change from year to year, indicating that Drew was not making progress. Drew's parents took him out of the public school and enrolled him in a private school specializing in the education of students with autism.

After a few months of intensive academic instruction and a comprehensive **behavior plan**, Drew's academic progress and behaviors greatly improved.

Drew's parents wanted him to attend his previous public school, so they approached Douglas County. They asked for an updated IEP to reflect the behavior plan and academic interventions that the private school was providing. When the school presented an IEP that Drew's parents believed to be essentially the same as his previous IEP, they placed Drew back in the private school and filed a due process complaint seeking reimbursement for tuition. Drew's parents argued that his IEP was not reasonably calculated for Drew to receive educational benefit. The hearing officer ruled the school's IEP did provide Drew with educational benefit; therefore, FAPE was provided, and tuition reimbursement to Drew's parents for the private school was denied.

Drew's parents appealed the decision. Ruling after ruling, the courts agreed with the school district that FAPE was provided to Drew despite his parents' request for an IEP with more **rigorous** special education services. In fact, the Tenth Circuit Court of Appeals stated in its ruling that based on the Rowley standard of a "basic floor of opportunity," Drew's IEP was calculated to provide educational benefit, even though it was "merely more than de minimis" (Brady et al., 2020). Drew's parents appealed the circuit court's decision and asked the U.S. Supreme Court to answer the following question: what is the level of educational benefit that school districts must provide children with disabilities in order to satisfy the free appropriate public education provision of IDEA?

In a unanimous Supreme Court ruling, the new standard of FAPE was "to meet the substantive obligation under IDEA, a school must offer an IEP reasonably calculated to enable a child to make progress appropriate in light of the child's circumstances" (*Endrew F. v. Douglas County School District*, 2017). The court rejected the de minimis standard applied by the Tenth Circuit Court and stated the new standard as markedly more demanding. Although the de minimis standard of educational benefit was rejected, the higher educational benefit standard applied by other circuit courts was also not adopted. The new standard requires hearing officers and judges to focus on the appropriateness of an IEP on a case-by-case basis and judge its adequacy in light of a child's circumstances. The Supreme Court did not overturn the *Rowley* decision, rather it amended the *Rowley* two-part test. The new Rowley/Endrew test is:

1. Has the school district complied with the procedures of the IDEA?
2. Is the IEP reasonably calculated to enable the student to make appropriate progress in light of the student's circumstances?

How do I ensure free appropriate public education?

Given the history of litigation concerning FAPE, educators and administrators should be well aware of the Rowley/Endrew test when determining whether

FAPE is being provided or not. Yell (2019) identified six principles that can guide school districts when developing appropriate programs for students with disabilities.

Principle 1: Involve parents in the IEP process. Within IDEA, Congress has asserted that a student's parents or guardians must participate in a full, equal, and meaningful way in the identification, assessment, programming, and placement of their child in special education. IDEA (2004) states,

> Almost thirty years of research and experience has demonstrated that the education of children with disabilities can be made more effective by strengthening the role and responsibility of parents and ensuring that families [. . .] have meaningful opportunities to participate in the education of their children.

As equal members of the IEP team, parents have the right to pursue FAPE for their child and participate in determining the components of their child's appropriate education.

Principle 2: Provide administrators, teachers, and staff training on their responsibilities under IDEA. Administrators and teachers who do not understand their obligations under IDEA may violate a student's procedural or substantive rights. It is important that all personnel involved in a child's special education and related services understand their responsibilities under IDEA. In particular, teachers must be fluent in evidence-based instructional practices and progress monitoring methods.

Principle 3: Develop educationally meaningful and legally sound IEPs. IEPs must be reasonably calculated to enable a child to make appropriate progress in light of their circumstances. School districts can ensure this is accomplished by using educational practices that show evidence of **efficacy** and implementing those practices with **fidelity**. Through the collection of student progress data, school personnel can adjust instruction based on whether the student is making academic and/or functional progress.

Principle 4: Provide access to the general education curriculum. Students in special education must have access to the general education curriculum. Given that their disability affects educational performance, the IEP must describe how their disability affects involvement in the general education curriculum. Annual goals and objectives within a student's IEP must, therefore, include instructional practices enabling access to the general curriculum based on the student's individual circumstances.

Principle 5: Place students in their least restrictive environment. IDEA mandates that students in special education are placed in their **least restrictive environment** (LRE; see chapter 5 for more about the LRE pillar of IDEA). This means students with disabilities should spend as much time as possible with their nondisabled peers. The IDEA mandate has two parts: (1) children with disabilities must be educated alongside children without disabilities to the maximum extent appropriate; and (2) the removal of children with disabilities from the general educational environment should occur only if the nature or severity of the disability is such that education in general education classes with the use of supplementary aids and services cannot be achieved satisfactorily. When determining a student's placement, the IEP team must account for the student's individual circumstances and what is, or is not, appropriate for that student to make educational progress.

Principle 6: Fully implement the IEP as written. The IEP is a legally binding, collaborative document that establishes a student's FAPE. All school personnel identified in a student's IEP (e.g., general education teachers, related service providers, etc.) must carry out their responsibilities as outlined by the IEP. An IEP is an agreement between the school and parents, and it is the school district's responsibility to implement the IEP as written.

Figure 4.2 provides a checklist school districts can use to ensure FAPE. Free education and public education are concepts of FAPE that generate less conflict than appropriate education. Although procedural FAPE is also a more

Free Education Requirements

☐ Parents or guardians are not charged for any special education or related services.
☐ Cost of service(s) were/are not considered when determining appropriateness.
☐ If two or more options are available for a particular program or service, and both will enable the student to make appropriate progress in light of the student's circumstances, the IEP team can consider cost.

Appropriate Procedural Requirements

☐ IDEA and state special education procedures were followed during the evaluation and IEP development.
☐ All procedures were conducted within statutory time frames.
☐ Parents were involved in a meaningful way in the development of their child's IEP and are involved in ongoing IEP meetings.
☐ All other relevant stakeholders were included in the evaluation and IEP developments and are involved in ongoing IEP meetings.
☐ Student progress is systematically monitored and regularly reported to parents.

Appropriate Substantive Requirements

☐ Annual IEP goals are ambitious, challenging, and measurable.
☐ Special education services are designed to enable the student to make appropriate progress in light of the student's circumstances.
☐ Special education services are clearly specified in the student's IEP.
☐ If progress monitoring data indicated student was not progressing toward his or her goals, instructional changes occurred.
☐ Assessments are relevant, meaningful, and address all of the student's needs.
☐ The IEP team can justify the decisions they made on a student's IEP regarding his or her progress.

Public Education Requirements

☐ Student with an IEP has access to a public preschool, elementary, and secondary education.
☐ Special education goals and objectives are aligned to state educational standards.

Figure 4.2 Checklist to Ensure FAPE.

straightforward determination, only close examination of a student's IEP can establish substantive FAPE. As we will discuss in chapter 6, the IEP is the cornerstone of a student's educational program and the blueprint of a student's FAPE.

Where can I find more information about free appropriate public education?

Wright's Law (www.wrightslaw.com). A comprehensive compilation of resources about various legal topics regarding special education. Browse relevant court cases, articles, books, and a questions and answers section about FAPE. To visit this resource follow this link: https://www.wrightslaw.com/info/fape.index.htm.

U.S. Department of Education. An official guidance document on the implications of the Endrew F. Supreme Court Decision reviews the facts of the Endrew F. case, clarifies the new FAPE standard, and provides considerations for implementation. The document can be found at https://sites.ed.gov/idea/files/qa-endrewcase-12-07-2017.pdf.

National Association of Special Education Teachers. The National Association of Special Education Teachers (NASET) is a national membership organization dedicated to rendering all possible support and assistance to those preparing for or teaching in the field of special education. NASET was founded to promote the profession of special education teachers and to provide a national forum for their ideas. NASET provides video courses on wide-ranging topics in special education. Membership of NASET is required to access the video lecture series. For the video course of Free and Appropriate Public Education visit https://www.naset.org/index.php?id=4902.

Key Terms

Behavior plan: A written course for what to do to prevent challenging behavior and what to do when it occurs. A behavior plan should specify a reinforcement and punishment system, as well as who is in charge of making revisions, and when the team will meet to discuss updates to the plan.

De minimis: A Latin expression meaning "about minimal things." De minimis educational benefit is slightly more than no educational benefit.

Due process hearing: Similar to a courtroom trial where both sides of a dispute can present evidence, call witnesses, and make legal arguments. A hearing officer or judge oversees the trial and makes a judgment.

Efficacy: Effectiveness or ability to accomplish the intended goal.

Fidelity: The extent to which delivery of an intervention adheres to the protocol or program model originally developed.

Individualized: Specific and unique to one's circumstances.

Least restrictive environment (LRE): A mandate in IDEA that students with disabilities should be educated to the maximum extent appropriate with their nondisabled peers.

Level of educational benefit: The degree to which one is expected to demonstrate functional and/or academic progress.

Objective: Defined; clear-cut; based on facts not opinions.

Procedural rights: Procedures that must be followed to ensure special education rights, as outlined in IDEA, are provided.

Related services: Transportation and such developmental, corrective, and other supportive services as are required to help a child with a disability benefit from special education.

Rigorous: Extremely thorough, exhaustive, and accurate.

Subjective: Ambiguous; not easily defined; interpreted with feelings and opinions.

Substantive rights: Protections of the content and quality of educational services.

Transition planning: Planning to promote successful movement from high school to post-school activities, such as postsecondary education, vocational training, employment, adult services, independent living, and community participation.

Discussion Questions

1. Did the Endrew F. Supreme Court decision clarify the level of educational benefit that school districts must provide children with disabilities in order to satisfy the free appropriate public education provision of IDEA?

2. How does FAPE relate to special education and the services provided?

3. What role do special education teachers play in ensuring FAPE is properly implemented?

4. How did *Board of Education of the Hendrick Hudson School District v. Rowley* (1982) impact the education of students with disabilities and how schools function today?

References

Bateman, B. D. (2017). Individualized education programs. In J. M. Kauffman and D. P. Hallahan (Eds.), *Handbook of special education*, 2nd ed., (pp. 91-124). Taylor & Francis/Routledge.

Board of Education of the Hendrick Hudson School District v. Rowley, 485 U.S. 176 (1982).

Brady, K. P., Russo, C. J., Dieterich, C. A., & Osborne Jr, A. G. (2020). *Legal issues in special education: Principles, policies, and practices*. Routledge.

Doe ex rel. Doe v. Bd. of Ed. of Tullahoma City Sch., 9 F.3d 455, 459-460 (6th Cir. 1993).

Endrew F. v. Douglas County School District, 137 S. Ct. 988 (2017).

Individuals with Disabilities Education Act of 2004, 20 U.S.C. § 1400.

Smith, R. C. (1996). *A case about Amy.* Temple University Press.

Wenkart, R. D. (2000). *Appropriate education for students with disabilities: How courts determine compliance with the IDEA.* LRP publications.

Yell, M. L. (2019). *The law and special education* (5th ed.). Pearson Education.

Yell, M. L., & Bateman, D. F. (2017). *Endrew F. v. Douglas County School District* (2017): FAPE and the Supreme Court. *Teaching Exceptional Children, 50,* 1-9.

Yell, M. L., Katsiyannis, A., Ennis, R. P., Losinski, M., & Christle, C. A. (2016). Avoiding substantive errors in individualized education program development. *Teaching Exceptional Children, 49,* 31-40. https://doi.org/10.1177/0040059916662204

CHAPTER 5

Nondiscriminatory Evaluation

> *Unfortunately, special education has a history of misidentifying students with disabilities based on racial and cultural characteristics. Nondiscriminatory evaluations are so important in ensuring that students receive the supports required based solely on their educational needs.*
>
> *Shelby Pavelka*
> *School Psychologist in Indiana*

The Individuals with Disabilities Education Act (IDEA) requires that before a student is placed in special education and afforded an individualized education program (IEP), they must be evaluated to determine whether they have a disability that affects educational performance. If a disability under IDEA is documented, the evaluation process also determines the nature and extent of the student's academic and functional needs that will be addressed in their IEP. The evaluation process is a critical component of IDEA and is necessary in establishing the appropriateness of a student's free appropriate public education right. In this chapter, we will discuss the second pillar of special education, nondiscriminatory evaluations (figure 5.1), and answer these essential questions:

1. What is a nondiscriminatory evaluation?
2. How does a nondiscriminatory evaluation relate to a free appropriate public education?
3. What regulations and court cases have defined a nondiscriminatory evaluation?
4. How do I ensure a nondiscriminatory evaluation?
5. Where can I find more information about appropriate evaluations?

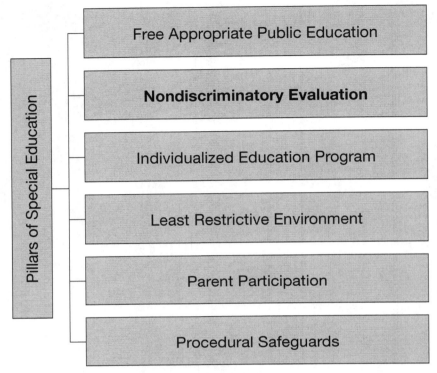

Figure 5.1 Nondiscriminatory Evaluation Is the Second Pillar of Special Education.

What is a nondiscriminatory evaluation?

In order for a student to become eligible for special education and related services, they must have a comprehensive evaluation. The evaluation will identify specific needs of the student and clarify whether those needs require special education services. The process may seem long, but it is one that ensures that only those students who actually need assistance are the ones receiving services. The evaluation process also ensures that students without disabilities are not placed in special education because they had a couple of bad days in the classroom. There are multiple checks and balances on the system confirming that a nondiscriminatory evaluation takes place. **Nondiscriminatory** means that the evaluation process is not biased for or against any individual or group of students.

In the past, school districts relied on evaluation assessments that were racially or culturally biased. In particular, intelligence quotient (IQ) assessments were **standardized** with populations of students that were not demographically representative of all students.

For the most part, assessments were standardized with scores of middle-to-upper-class white, male students. Assessment question scores that might be less familiar to a student with different experiences, for example, a Latina girl from a lower income household, would not be represented within standardized

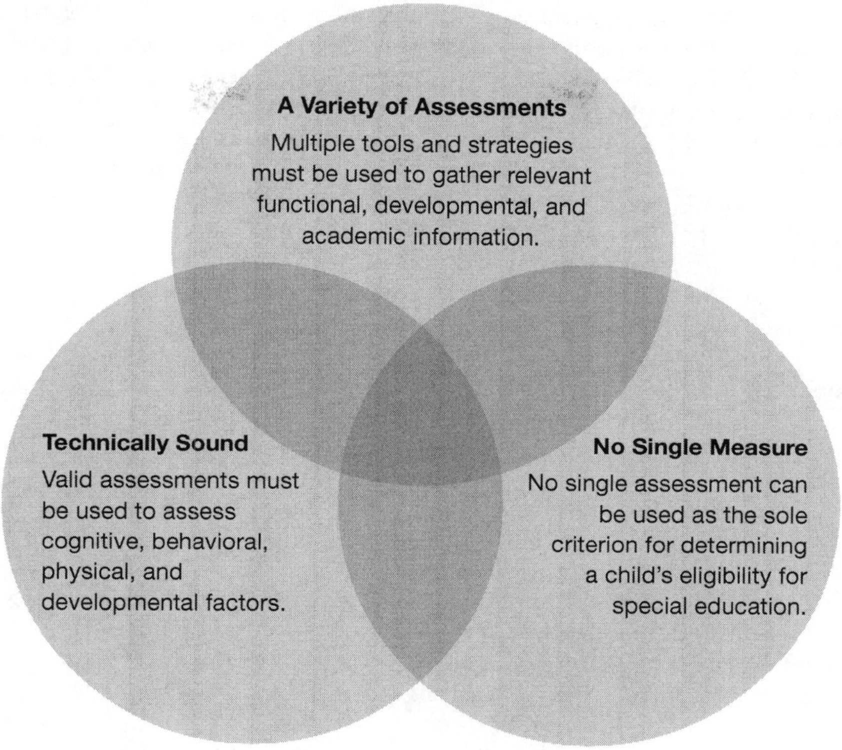

A Variety of Assessments

Multiple tools and strategies must be used to gather relevant functional, developmental, and academic information.

Technically Sound

Valid assessments must be used to assess cognitive, behavioral, physical, and developmental factors.

No Single Measure

No single assessment can be used as the sole criterion for determining a child's eligibility for special education.

Figure 5.2 Venn Diagram of the Three Components of a Nondiscriminatory Evaluation (IDEA, 2004).

scores. The girl may score lower on the IQ assessment, not because of her intelligence but simply because the test was designed and standardized for different students.

Discriminatory evaluations became a particular concern in special education due to the **overrepresentation** of minority students or students from economically disadvantaged backgrounds (Yell, 2019). Too often, IQ assessments were relied on solely to make special education placement decisions. To remedy overrepresentation, IDEA, case law, and regulatory laws have provided guidance over the years. In 2004, IDEA was amended to enhance the rules and procedures for conducting nondiscriminatory evaluations. Figure 5.2 presents three key components of a nondiscriminatory evaluation.

How does a nondiscriminatory evaluation relate to a free appropriate public education?

All school districts have an obligation to seek out and identify eligible students who have a disability that would require special education and related services. This obligation is often referred to as the **child-find** obligation.

Child find is an important legal component of special education and is the first step to ensuring that a student receives a free appropriate public education (FAPE). In order for a student to receive FAPE, they must be identified as requiring special education services. Under Part B (for children three to twenty-one) and Part C (for children from birth through age two) of IDEA, states must proactively seek out and identify children with disabilities. State government and school personnel cannot sit back and wait for students with disabilities to be referred for evaluations. Child-find programs may include a multitude of strategies to identify children with disabilities, such as screenings at pediatrician's offices, public awareness programs, television and radio advertisements, and coordinated activities with other local service providers (Zirkel, 2015). Once a child is identified as having a potential disability through child find, they are not automatically eligible for special education services. Children who are located through the child-find process must enter the nondiscriminatory evaluation process within a reasonable period of time (Zirkel, 2015).

As discussed in previous chapters, FAPE consists of two types of requirements: procedural and substantive. Nondiscriminatory evaluations relate to FAPE within these two requirement types as well. First, we will discuss the procedural requirements of a nondiscriminatory evaluation that relate to FAPE.

Procedural requirements of a nondiscriminatory evaluation. IDEA 2004 includes language that allows school district personnel, a parent, or another state agency to initiate a request for an initial evaluation. Once a request for an evaluation has been received by the school, the school must meet to determine if an evaluation is warranted. If an evaluation is necessary, the school must conduct a full and individual evaluation before the initial provision of special education and related services to a child with a disability (IDEA, 2004). The regulations are very specific about the process and how an evaluation should occur. We will first discuss the broad evaluation procedures and then discuss the specifics related to students with learning disabilities, as there are special rules for this disability category.

First, it is imperative that a school district notify the child's parent (in writing) and receive consent before an evaluation begins. As we will introduce in chapter 6, and further explore in chapter 8, parents are essential members of a student's IEP team and must be included in the decision-making process. After parental consent is provided to conduct an initial evaluation, the three components of a nondiscriminatory evaluation must be adhered to (figure 5.2). In addition to the nondiscriminatory components, procedural requirements also entail the following:

- The evaluation is administered by trained and knowledgeable personnel.
- Assessments are administered in accordance with any instructions provided by the producer of the assessments.
- Assessments are selected and administered so as to best ensure that if an assessment is administered to a child with impaired sensory, manual, or speaking skills, the assessment results accurately reflect the child's aptitude or achievement level or whatever other factors the test purports to measure,

rather than reflecting the child's impaired sensory, manual, or speaking skills (unless those skills are the factors that the test purports to measure).

- The child is assessed in all areas related to the suspected disability, including, if appropriate, health, vision, hearing, social and emotional status, general intelligence, academic performance, communicative status, and motor abilities.
- Assessments are provided and administered in the child's native language or another mode of communication and in the form most likely to yield accurate information on what the child knows and can do academically, developmentally, and functionally.
- Assessments of children with disabilities who transfer from one public agency to another public agency in the same school year are coordinated with those children's prior and subsequent schools, as necessary and as expeditiously as possible to ensure prompt completion of full evaluations.

The reauthorization of IDEA in 2004 changed the manner in which students were identified for the category of learning disabilities. Previously, schools used the **discrepancy model** to determine whether a student had a specific learning disability by comparing the student's intellectual ability and academic achievement (Murawski & Scott, 2017).

If the student's IQ indicated average intelligence, yet the student was academically performing significantly below their age-appropriate peers, then a discrepancy was noted, and the student may qualify for special education services. Many critiques of the discrepancy model have emerged since its codification in law in 1977 (U.S. Office of Education, 1977). The most common critique was that the deficit model of identification caused a wait-to-fail approach to the identification of disability and subsequent provision of special education services (Kavale & Flanagan, 2007). The discrepancy between a student's IQ and achievement could not be identified until only after a substantial amount of time passed. A student was required, therefore, to struggle academically for a long enough period until a significant deficit occurred between their IQ and academic ability. Often, this meant a student would struggle academically for years until they qualified for special education services.

In 2004, IDEA was amended with the following criteria for determining whether a child has a specific learning disability:

- States must not require the use of a severe discrepancy between intellectual ability and achievement for determining whether a child has a specific learning disability.
- States must permit the use of a process based on the child's response to scientific, research-based intervention.
- States may permit the use of other alternative research-based procedures for determining whether a child has a specific learning disability.

Response to intervention (RTI) became the new model for identifying a specific learning disability.

RTI is a means of providing early intervention to all students at risk for school failure (Fuchs & Fuchs, 2006). Rather than waiting for a student to fail,

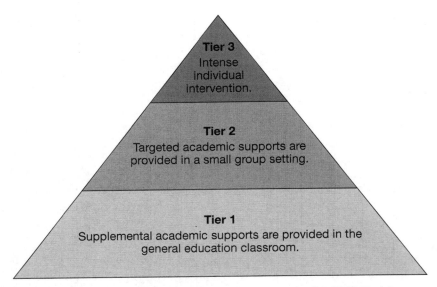

Figure 5.3 Levels of Support within the Response to Intervention (RTI) Model.

levels of academic support are systematically increased and then monitored to see if the student responds positively to the support. Figure 5.3 visually represents the tiers of support that are provided in an RTI model. A student who does not respond positively to the academic supports provided in tier one will be moved into tier two. After a reasonable amount of time and detailed **progress monitoring,** if the student does not respond positively to the targeted support, they will move into tier three.

Within tier three the student will receive an evaluation for special education. According to IDEA (2004) a specific learning disability diagnosis is determined when:

- The student does not make sufficient progress to meet age or State-approved grade-level standards when using a process based on the child's response to scientific, research-based intervention; or
- The student exhibits a pattern of strengths and weaknesses in performance, achievement, or both, relative to age or intellectual development, that is determined by the group to be relevant to the identification of a specific learning disability, using appropriate assessments, and are not primarily the result of:
  - A visual, hearing, or motor disability
  - Intellectual disability
  - Emotional disturbance
  - Cultural factors
  - Environmental or economic disadvantage
  - Limited English proficiency

As you can see, the determination of a specific learning disability is also about eliminating other reasons for poor academic achievement. In addition, to ensure that underachievement in a student suspected of having a specific learning disability is not due to lack of **appropriate instruction** in reading or math, an evaluation must demonstrate that prior to the evaluation the student was provided appropriate instruction in regular education settings, delivered by qualified personnel.

The final procedural requirement we should mention is that all eligible students must be reevaluated at least every three years. A triennial evaluation is to determine whether the student still needs special education. Specifically, the triennial evaluation answers these questions:

* Does the student have a disability?
* Does the student have educational needs related to their disability?

The triennial evaluation functions similarly to the initial evaluation in that it determines eligibility. The law requires students eligible for special education to be reevaluated at least every three years, but the student may be reevaluated more often if the parent or the student's teacher(s) request it. Some states require within their specific special education legislation that certain disability categories receive biannual evaluations (e.g., students identified with intellectual disabilities in Pennsylvania). Although states require legislative provisions above and beyond federal legislation, states cannot do less than federal requirements.

Procedural requirements related to an evaluation and FAPE are fairly straightforward. However, the second important part of a nondiscriminatory evaluation is the substantive requirements. Does the evaluation do what is necessary to get a clear understanding of the needs of the student in order to first determine eligibility and, second, to determine the appropriate programming and placement for the student?

Substantive requirements of a nondiscriminatory evaluation. In addition to determining eligibility, the evaluation must also be used to determine the student's educational needs. The initial evaluation is one of the most important parts in developing a student's IEP and determining the appropriateness of a student's FAPE. Information from a student's initial evaluation serves as the basis for the student's special education program. It serves as the basis for eligibility, addresses any goals and accommodations the student will need, and helps determine the level or amount of services necessary for the student. As Salvia et al. (2017) describe, an assessment (i.e., evaluation) is the process of collecting information for the purpose of making decisions about students. In previous chapters, we have covered in great detail the subjectivity of the term "appropriate." The. *Endrew F. v. Douglas County School District* (2017) Supreme Court decision helped clarify the definition of "appropriate" by stating that in order "to meet the substantive obligation under IDEA, a school must offer an IEP reasonably calculated to enable a child to make progress appropriate in light of the child's circumstances." In chapter 6 we will discuss the process of developing a "reasonably calculated" IEP that starts with accurate present levels of academic achievement and functional performance (PLAAFP) statements. An initial nondiscriminatory evaluation is where the IEP team establishes a student's PLAAFP.

What regulations and court cases have defined a nondiscriminatory evaluation?

Statutory amendments to IDEA since its original passage in 1975 have changed the evaluation process. As previously discussed, the discrepancy model of evaluation for students with specific learning disabilities was replaced by the RTI model in 2004. Apart from statutory changes to IDEA, however, other important regulations and court cases have defined a nondiscriminatory evaluation.

Larry P. v. Riles (1979). The first significant court case that affected evaluations was heard at a federal district court in California. In *Larry P. v. Riles* (1979, hereinafter *Larry P.*) five African American children, who had been placed in special education classes for the "educable mentally retarded" (i.e., intellectually disabled [ID]), filed suit in the Federal District Court of Northern California claiming that they had been wrongly placed in special education based on their performance on intelligence tests that were racially biased and discriminatory. The lawsuit also claimed that a disproportionate number of black students were placed in ID classes compared to other students. The federal court ruled in favor of the plaintiffs and prohibited the use of IQ tests to identify or place black students in ID classes. The decision was appealed to the Ninth Circuit Court of Appeals in 1984 and upheld. The circuit court expanded the ruling by banning the use of IQ tests for all African American students who have been referred for special education.

Crawford v. Honig (1994). The *Crawford v. Honig* (1994) lawsuit was brought to the Ninth Circuit Court of Appeals to challenge the *Larry P.* ruling. A group of African American students requested IQ tests be allowed for determining the eligibility of black students to receive special education services under the category of learning disabilities (Powers et al., 2004). At that time, the discrepancy model was used to determine whether a student had a learning disability. The use of IQ tests was necessary to identify a discrepancy between IQ and academic achievement. The ban on IQ tests from the *Larry P.* ruling was preventing the proper identification of African American students with learning disabilities. In *Crawford v. Honig* the court agreed with the plaintiffs and vacated the *Larry P.* ban on IQ tests for identifying African American students with learning disabilities. The ban on IQ tests, however, remained in place for identifying African American students with intellectual disabilities.

Timothy W. v. Rochester, N. H. School District (1989). Timothy was born premature and had numerous severe developmental disabilities. When Timothy reached school age, his school conducted an initial evaluation. Although the school identified Timothy as having multiple disabilities under IDEA, the school determined that he was not "capable of benefiting" from an education (Brady et al., 2020). The primary legal issue of the *Timothy W.* case involved whether a school can deny a child with a disability an education based on the child being "uneducable." The First Circuit Court of Appeals ruled in favor of Timothy and affirmed what is known as the **"zero reject"** principle of IDEA. The zero reject principle essentially states that no child, regardless of disability severity, can be denied special education services.

The *Timothy W.* decision also defined education in a broader sense to encompass nonacademic and functional skills to educate a child for basic life skills (Brady et al., 2020).

How do I ensure a nondiscriminatory evaluation?

We recommend the following steps as guidance for an appropriate and nondiscriminatory evaluation.

1. Draw on information from a variety of sources, including aptitude and achievement tests, teacher recommendations, physical condition, social or cultural background, and adaptive behavior. In other words, no single assessment can determine placement. The team needs to use multiple data points in making any eligibility determination.
2. Ensure all evaluation data are documented and carefully considered. All the information presented must be considered. The evaluation team should also document their comments about the information and be able to note that they considered every aspect.
3. Ensure decisions are made by a team, including a person knowledgeable about the student, the meaning of the evaluation data, and the placement options. Typically, an evaluation team will have a school psychologist who conducts most of the assessments, but this also means that the decision is based on every team member having the opportunity to participate and share their viewpoints. Make sure the parents are included as a part of the team, and their statements regarding the student's needs are included and fully considered.
4. Ensure the placement decision is made in accordance with least restrictive environment (LRE) requirements. After a student is found eligible under IDEA, work to make sure all programming provided for the student allows for participation in the general education classroom for the maximum possible amount, including participation with nondisabled peers in all school-related activities, such as transportation, lunch, specials, and extracurricular activities.
5. Ensure a point person is assigned to address any questions the parents have about the process, and that the team should meet if there is additional information provided or there are problems with the student's initial individualized education program (IEP) or placement.

A nondiscriminatory evaluation is the foundation of a student's FAPE. An IEP can only be reasonably calculated in light of the student's circumstances following a relevant and meaningful evaluation. As Bateman (2017) wrote, "the

IEP must stand solidly and squarely on a foundation of current, accurate evaluations of the student's level of performance in academic and functional areas" (p. 93). A nondiscriminatory evaluation is the second pillar of IDEA because it is a critical component in the identification and development of special education services for students with disabilities.

Where can I find more information about nondiscriminatory evaluations?

Center for Parent Information & Resources (www.parentcenterhub.org). A central "hub" of information and products created for the network of parent centers serving families of children with disabilities. This website provides an overview of information for evaluating school-aged children for a disability: https://www.parentcenterhub.org/evaluation/.

IDEA Basics: Eligibility and Diagnosis. In this video, a special education advocate and special education attorney discuss the important distinction between medical diagnosis of a disability and eligibility for special education under IDEA. The short video (4:25) is geared toward parents of children with disabilities and helping them understand common terminology used in special education: https://www.youtube.com/watch?v=1A4WxH_wu-0.

Understood (www.understood.org). Understood is a non-profit dedicated to serving the millions of families of kids who learn and think differently. Understood is dedicated to growing and shaping a world where everyone who learns and thinks differently feels supported at home, at school, and at work; a world where people with all types of disabilities have the opportunity to enjoy meaningful careers; a world where more communities embrace differences. This page outlines the rights afforded to parents of children with disabilities during the evaluation process: https://www.understood.org/en/school-learning/your -childs-rights/evaluation-rights/evaluation-rights-what-you-need-to-know.

Key Terms

Appropriate instruction: Scientific and evidence-based instruction.
Child find: A program, mandated by IDEA, that requires states to continuously search for and evaluate children who may have a disability.
Discrepancy model: Determination of a learning disability by comparing IQ and academic achievement.
Nondiscriminatory: Not biased for or against any individual or group of students.
Overrepresentation: Representation of a group in a category that exceeds expectation for that group.
Progress monitoring: Scheduled data collection to monitor a student's progress toward a goal.

Response to intervention: Determination of a learning disability by measuring a student's response to increased levels of academic support.

Standardized: Calibrated in a manner to allow comparisons of relative performance of one individual to a group of individuals.

Zero reject: A component of the child-find provision in IDEA that ensures no child can be denied a free appropriate public education regardless of severity of disability.

Discussion Questions

1. Discuss the pros and cons of each model (discrepancy and response to intervention) for determining eligibility under IDEA for a learning disability.

2. Should California maintain the ban on using IQ assessments to determine whether black students qualify for special education under the intellectual disability category of IDEA?

3. What are some child-find programs within your state and local district?

4. Why are the procedural and substantive requirements of a nondiscriminatory evaluation so important?

References

Bateman, B. D. (2017). *Individualized education programs for children with disabilities.* In J. M. Kauffman & D. P. Hallahan (Eds.), *The handbook of special education* (2nd ed., pp. 91-112). Routledge.

Brady, K. P., Russo, C. J., Dieterich, C. A., & Osborne Jr, A. G. (2019). *Legal issues in special education: Principles, policies, and practices.* Routledge.

Crawford v. Honig, 37 F.3d 485 (9th Cir. 1994).

Fuchs, D., & Fuchs, L. S. (2006). Introduction to response to intervention: What, why, and how valid is it? *Reading Research Quarterly, 41*(1), 93-99.

Individuals with Disabilities Education Act of 2004, 20 U.S.C. § 1400.

Kavale, K. A., & Flanagan, D. P. (2007). Ability—achievement discrepancy, response to intervention, and assessment of cognitive abilities/processes in specific learning disability identification: Toward a contemporary operational definition. In *Handbook of response to intervention* (pp. 130-147). Springer.

Larry P. v. Riles, 495 F. Supp. 926 (N.D. Cal. 1979).

Murawski, W. W. & Scott, K. L. (2017). *What really works with exceptional learners.* Corwin Publishing.

Powers, K. M., Hagans-Murillo, K. S., & Restori, A. F. (2004). Twenty-five years after Larry P: The California response to overrepresentation of African Americans in special education. *The California School Psychologist, 9*(1), 145-158. https://doi.org/10.1007/BF03340915.

Salvia, J., Ysseldyke, J. E., & Witmer, S. (2017). *Assessment in special and inclusive education* (13th ed.). Cengage.

Timothy W. v. Rochester, N. H. School District, 875 F.2d 954 (1st Cir. 1989).

U.S. Office of Education (1977). Assistance to states for education of handicapped children: Procedures for evaluating specific learning disabilities. *Federal Register, 42*(250), 65082–65085. Washington, DC: U.S. Government Printing Office.

Yell, M. L. (2019). *The law and special education* (5th ed.). Pearson Education.

Zirkel, P. A. (2015). Special education law: Illustrative basics and nuances of key IDEA components. *Teacher Education and Special Education, 38*(4), 263-275.

CHAPTER 6

Individualized Education Program

> *An IEP tells the educational story of the child, serving as a roadmap for the provision of special education services and supports.*
>
> Angela L. Balsley, EdD
> President of the Indiana Council for Administrators
> of Special Education

Special education is specially designed instruction to meet the unique needs of students with disabilities (IDEA, 2004). It is grounded in a belief that all students deserve access and accountability in education to improve their quality of life. Now that special education has been a part of the educational system for close to half a century (since the Education of All Handicapped Children Act [EAHCA] of 1975), society generally champions the rights and inclusion of people with disabilities. Agreeing with a philosophical concept is one thing; taking that concept and applying it to millions of students with disabilities across this country in schools and classrooms is a more difficult task. Congress, therefore, developed the individualized education program (IEP) as the method of implementing special education. A student's IEP is the cornerstone to their special education success. As we will learn, an IEP is more than a document; it is a process and product of special education that guides and materializes the belief that all children deserve a free appropriate public education (FAPE). In this chapter we will discuss the third pillar of special education, IEPs (figure 6.1), and answer these essential questions:

1. What is an individualized education program?
2. How does an individualized education program relate to free appropriate public education?
3. What regulations and court cases have defined the individualized education program?

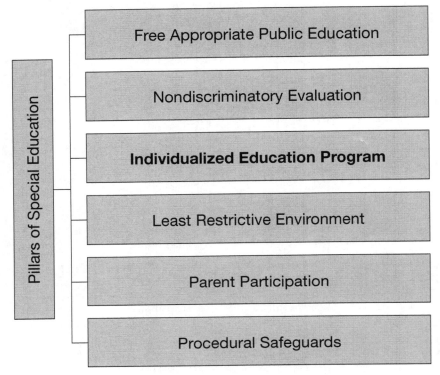

Figure 6.1 Individualized Education Program Is the Third Pillar of Special Education.

4. How do I develop a legally compliant individualized education program?
5. Where can I find more information about individualized education programs?

What is an individualized education program?

An IEP is both a process and a product that is outlined in IDEA (2004). There are procedural requirements guiding the process when developing an IEP, and there are substantive requirements establishing the contents of an IEP. Procedural and substantive requirements must be adhered to by school personnel, or else an IEP may be rendered inappropriate and thus a violation of a student's free appropriate public education (FAPE).

Procedural requirements. An IEP is developed in a planning process where school personnel and parents collaborate to create a program of special education and related services. Prior to developing the IEP, however, there are basic steps that must occur if a student is believed to have a disability that is negatively affecting their education. Figure 6.2 outlines the five-step process from special education referral to IEP development.

First, a student that is believed to have a disability is referred to a **multidisciplinary team (MDT)**.

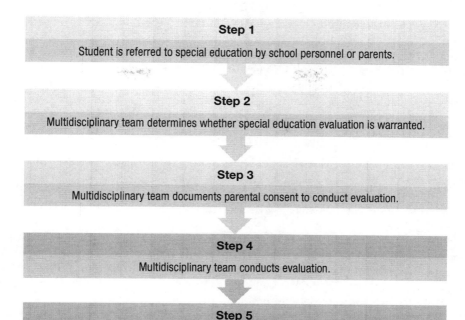

Figure 6.2 The IEP Process.

An MDT consists of school personnel such as a school psychologist, school counselor, school nurse, special educator, and others as needed. Typically, school personnel such as a general education teacher will refer a student for special education services since they are the ones most closely working with and documenting the student's academic progress. Sometimes, though, parents that suspect their child has a disability will refer their child for special education. After considering the special education referral and examining preliminary student data, the MDT decides whether a special education evaluation is warranted. If the MDT believes an evaluation is required to determine whether a student qualifies for special education services, the team must document parental consent to conduct the evaluation. If the student's parents agree to have their child evaluated for special education services, the MDT conducts an evaluation (the essentials of a nondiscriminatory evaluation are discussed in chapter 5).

If the results of the nondiscriminatory evaluation determine the student *does not* qualify for special education services, the process stops. An IEP is not developed and the student remains in their current setting without special education and related services. The school should, however, consider why the student was referred for special education and whether any instructional strategies and support can be adopted to address the initial concerns. If the results of the nondiscriminatory evaluation determine the student *does* qualify for special education services, then an IEP team is formed.

IDEA (2004) identifies those who are required to be on an IEP team as well as those who are permitted, but not required. The IEP team members who are required are: (a) the student's parents or legal guardians, (b) at least one special education teacher, (c) at least one general education teacher, (d) a representative from the local educational agency that is qualified to provide or supervise the special education program (usually the school principal), and (e) the child, when appropriate (required for a transition IEP). The IEP team members who are permitted but not required are those who bring additional expertise to the team depending on the student's individual needs, such as an assistive technology expert, or who provide related services to the student, such as the student's therapist.

After the IEP team has been formed, the next step is developing the IEP. It is critical that the student's parents or legal guardians are full participants in the IEP development process. IDEA regulations specifically outline requirements to ensure parental participation (Yell et al., 2013). These requirements include giving parents sufficient notice of the IEP meeting (ten days in advance) and holding the meeting at a mutually agreeable time and location (Yell, 2019). If inadequate efforts are made by school personnel to notify parents or schedule an IEP meeting at an acceptable time and location, the failure may result in a denial of FAPE (Bateman, 2017). In fact, parent participation is so important that the concept is one of the six pillars of special education. The essentials of parent participation will be covered in chapter 8.

Substantive requirements. Developing an IEP requires that the IEP team address, at a minimum, eight main components (see table 6.1). These eight

---

TABLE 6.1   Main Components of an IEP

1. A statement of the student's present levels of academic achievement and functional performance.
2. A statement of the student's measurable annual goals and short-term objectives.
3. A statement of how the student's progress toward meeting those goals will be measured and when progress will be reported to the student's parents.
4. A statement of the special education, related services, and supplemental aids and services that will be provided to the student.
5. An examination and statement of the extent to which the student will not participate in the general education classroom.
6. A statement of necessary accommodations for the student to participate in state-wide academic assessments; or a statement of how an alternative assessment was selected.
7. A statement of measurable postsecondary goals based on age-appropriate transition services (must be included for students who are 16 years old or older; state laws may require transition goals for students 14 or 15 years old or older).
8. The projected date for beginning special education services and the anticipated duration of the IEP.

components combine to create the product (i.e., written document) of a student's IEP. The rigor in developing and implementing the substance of an IEP is equally important as following the procedural requirements.

To start, a student's present levels of academic achievement and functional performance (PLAAFP) must be assessed and stated in the IEP. A description of the student's performance should provide a **baseline**, or clear picture, of current circumstances, including any academic or functional needs that affect the student's education (Harmon et al., 2020).

An accurate and thorough assessment of the student's PLAAFP allows the IEP team to develop goals and objectives.

The second component of an IEP is determining measurable annual goals and short-term objectives. In other words, where does the IEP team want the student to be **academically** and **functionally** in one year?

The annual goal establishes an end target, while short-term objectives allow the IEP team to document the student's progress along the way. Substantial research has explored the quality of IEP goals and objectives with general consensus identifying specific, measurable, attainable, relevant, and time-bound (SMART) goals as most effective (Goran et al., 2020; Hedin & DeSpain, 2018). At the end of this chapter, under *Where can I find more information about individualized education programs?* we provide a link to an online module that comprehensively discusses the process of writing SMART IEP goals.

After SMART IEP goals have been developed, the IEP team must identify how the student's progress toward meeting those goals will be measured and when progress will be reported to the student's parents. Regular **progress monitoring** is critical because it (a) keeps parents involved as collaborating participants in their child's education and (b) allows the IEP team to collect, analyze, and report data to determine if the special education support and related services are working as intended or not.

If the student is making adequate progress toward their annual goal and meeting short-term objectives, then great! The IEP team can continue as planned. If, however, the student is not making adequate progress as outlined by short-term objectives, then the IEP team should meet and discuss necessary support and service changes to provide greater educational benefit. Systematic progress monitoring is an essential substantive requirement that shows a data-based, data-driven IEP is reasonably calculated to enable the student to make progress appropriate in light of their circumstances.

After the goals are stated, the IEP team must determine the special education services, related services, and supplemental aids and services that will be provided to the student. Each need identified in the student's PLAAFP must be addressed by one of these services. Solely, or in combination, the services identified in this section of the IEP are the actions the school will take to enable the student to make progress in light of their circumstances.

Special education. A student who requires special education services should be provided **specially designed instruction (SDI)**. SDI is defined as

adapting, as appropriate to the needs of an eligible child, the content, methodology, or delivery of instruction to address the unique needs of the child that result from the child's disability and to ensure access of the child to the general curriculum, so that the child can meet the educational standards within the jurisdiction of the public agency that apply to all children. (34 C.F.R. § 300.39[b][3])

Related services. Related services allow a student to benefit from special education. Federal IDEA regulations (2012) define related services as

Supportive services [. . .] [including] speech-language pathology and audiology services, interpreting services, psychological services, physical and occupational therapy, recreation, including therapeutic recreation, early identification and assessment of disabilities in children, counseling services, including rehabilitation counseling, orientation and mobility services, and medical services for diagnostic or evaluation purposes. Related services also include school health services and school nurse services, social work services in schools, and parent counseling and training. (34 C.F.R. § 300.34[a])

Supplemental aids and services. Supplemental aids and services are "aids, services, and other supports that are provided in regular classes, other education-related settings, and in extracurricular and nonacademic settings, to enable students with disabilities to be educated with students without disabilities to the maximum extent appropriate" (34 C.F.R. § 300.42). Examples of supplemental aids and services may involve special seating arrangements for the student, using professional or student tutors, or working with the student's parents to help the child at home.

After a student's goals are drafted and services to meet those goals identified, the IEP team must determine the student's least restrictive environment (LRE) to receive those services. In doing so, the IEP team decides the extent to which the student *will not* participate in the general education classroom (see chapter 7 for the essentials of LRE). A student's LRE can only be determined on an individual basis because each student's PLAAFP, goals, and services are unique. Remember that a student's LRE placement is not a physical location; rather it is a point along the continuum of alternative placement options where the student will receive special education and related services (Federal Register, 2006). Given the continuum of alternative placement options, however, the LRE mandate in IDEA (2004) requires that children with disabilities be educated alongside children without disabilities to the *maximum extent appropriate.*

The sixth substantive component of the IEP is a statement of necessary accommodations for the student to participate in state-wide academic assessments, or a statement of how an alternative assessment was selected. A result of No Child Left Behind (2001), now the Every Student Succeeds Act (2015), was that students with disabilities were also included in school accountability assessments. States provide a list of accommodations to assist students with disabilities who are administered state academic assessments (e.g., extended time, testing in a separate location). For students with more severe disabilities, however, states are required to provide an alternative assessment that is based on modified or alternative academic standards.

If a student is old enough (sixteen or older), their IEP must include a statement of measurable postsecondary goals based on age-appropriate transition services (some state laws require transition goals for students as young as thirteen years old). Postsecondary goals and transition services are to help a student and their family prepare for life after school. The purpose of including transition services several years before a student ages out of IDEA protections is to (a) create a longer-term outlook into the IEP process; (b) assist each student in making a meaningful transition from the school setting to a post-school setting, which could include higher education, employment, or independent living; and (c) help students better reach their potential as adults (Prince et al., 2014).

Lastly, an IEP must include the projected date for beginning special education services and the anticipated duration of the IEP. The IEP must be implemented as soon as possible after it is written. In terms of duration, the IEP must be reviewed at least once a year (Office of Special Education Programs, 2000).

How does an individualized education program relate to free appropriate public education?

When Congress passed the EAHCA (1975), all students with disabilities who were eligible under the law were to receive a program of special education and related services that conferred FAPE. Although FAPE remains the centerpiece of the law (see chapter 4 on the essentials of FAPE), the IEP is the means by which a student's FAPE is developed and delivered (Bateman, 2017). A student's FAPE is realized within their IEP because all aspects of the student's special education are led and monitored throughout the IEP process (Smith, 1990). Both the procedural and substantive requirements of IDEA, which establish the appropriateness of a student's FAPE, are reflected in the procedural and substantive requirements of the IEP.

The congressional authors of the EAHCA (1975) and subsequent court rulings never sought to define a level of academic or functional progress for students to achieve in order to receive FAPE. The Supreme Court in *Board of Education of the Hendrick Hudson School District v. Rowley* (hereinafter *Rowley*, 1982) established, and recently reaffirmed in *Endrew F. v. Douglas County School District* (hereinafter *Endrew*, 2017), that there is no standard of progress that is applicable to all students. The very nature of IDEA (2004) is to provide individualized instruction and related services to meet each student's unique needs based on their PLAAFP. In fact, the Supreme Court has stated that to meet the substantive requirement of FAPE, a student's IEP must be reasonably calculated to enable them to make progress appropriate in light of their circumstances (*Endrew*, 2017). The IEP is "the primary evidence of the appropriateness of the child's educational program—its development, implementation and efficacy" (Bateman, 2017, p. 87).

What regulations and court cases have defined the individualized education program?

As discussed in chapter 4, *Rowley* (1982) and *Endrew* (2017) were seminal cases in defining FAPE. Because a student's FAPE is realized in the procedural and substantive requirements of their IEP, the two-part Rowley/Endrew test has helped define the IEP. The two-part test is as follows:

1. Has the school district complied with the procedures of the IDEA?
2. Is the IEP reasonably calculated to enable the student to make appropriate progress in light of the student's circumstances?

Case law has shown that procedural violations in the IEP process may invalidate an IEP. According to Yell (2019), for a court to rule an IEP invalid, however, the procedural violation must be more than trivial and have (a) compromised a student's right to an appropriate education, (b) resulted in excluding parents from the IEP process, or (c) caused the student to be deprived of educational rights. The most common procedural violation involves parental participation (Zirkel & Hetrick, 2017). In *Amanda J. v. Clark County School District* (2001), the U.S. Court of Appeals for the Ninth Circuit emphasized the importance of parental involvement:

> Among the most important procedural safeguards are those that protect the parents' right to be involved in the development of their child's educational plan. Parents not only represent the best interests of their child in the IEP development process, they also provide information about the child critical to developing a comprehensive IEP and which only they are in a position to know. (p. 878)

The second part of the Rowley/Endrew test addresses the substantive requirements of an IEP. The only way for a court to evaluate whether an IEP has been reasonably calculated to enable the student to make appropriate progress in light of their circumstances is to examine the content of the IEP (as listed in table 6.1). Based on the examination of that content, one can determine whether the IEP is reasonably calculated and whether it can confer appropriate progress in light of the student's circumstances.

The IEP is a legal document. It is a contract signed by a school district and the parents of a student with a disability. The written contract details a school district's promise to provide special education and related services to a particular student in order to ensure that the student receives FAPE (Lake, 2007). Remember that an IEP is a promise of resources and services; it is not a guarantee of student performance. As a legal contract, however, the school is required to implement the IEP as written in **good-faith effort**.

The concept of good-faith effort stems from contract law and is defined as "what a reasonable person would determine is a diligent and honest effort under the same set of facts or circumstances" (*AquaSource Inc. v. Wind Dance Farm, Inc.* 2005, para. 541). The school, therefore, must make good-faith efforts to implement a student's IEP and make good-faith efforts in assisting the student to achieve the goals outlined in the IEP.

How do I develop a legally compliant individualized education program?

The U.S. Supreme Court has directed hearing officers and lower courts to review a school's IEP process and product to determine whether a violation of FAPE has occurred. Using the Rowley/Endrew two-part test, courts are to first examine the procedural aspects of the IEP process. Second, they are to examine the IEP document itself to determine whether the IEP was reasonably calculated to enable the student to make progress appropriate in light of the student's circumstances. The following guidelines can help an IEP team meet the requirements of IDEA and develop a legally compliant IEP.

Procedural guidelines. There are three important guidelines to consider when procedurally developing an IEP (see figure 6.3). First, the IEP must make every effort to involve parents in all aspects of the IEP process—including evaluation, formulation, implementation, and review. Federal IDEA regulations require schools to (a) provide adequate notice of an IEP meeting; (b) schedule the IEP meeting at a mutually agreed upon time and place; (c) inform the parents of the purpose, time, and place of the meeting, and who will attend; and (d) inform the parents of their right to bring others of their choice to the meeting (34 C.F.R. § 300.322). Even though parents are essential members of the IEP team, this does not mean that they can dictate educational decisions. As members of the team, they should be asked to contribute, and their ideas should be discussed. Final educational decisions must come from mutual agreement and compromise between all members of the IEP team.

The second procedural guideline is to ensure the IEP team is composed of the legally required members. Lake (2002) argued that if an IEP is the cornerstone of IDEA, then the IEP team members, who have the task of developing the IEP, are the bricklayers of the program. Absent members from the IEP team create an inadequate team, thus the resulting IEP may prove to be inadequate as well. IDEA (2004) mandates the IEP team includes at least (a) the student's parents or legal guardians, (b) one special education teacher, (c) one general education teacher, and (d) a representative from the local educational agency that is qualified to provide or supervise the special education program (usually the school principal), and (e) the child, when appropriate (required for a transition IEP).

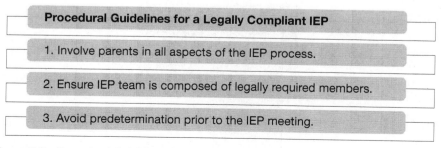

Procedural Guidelines for a Legally Compliant IEP

1. Involve parents in all aspects of the IEP process.

2. Ensure IEP team is composed of legally required members.

3. Avoid predetermination prior to the IEP meeting.

Figure 6.3 Procedural Guidelines for a Legally Compliant IEP.

Third, the IEP team must avoid predetermination prior to the IEP meeting. Predetermination is when school personnel make a final decision about a student's special education service or placement before the actual IEP meeting. If predetermination occurs, parents, or other attending members, have been denied any meaningful input into the decision. A judge in *Doyle v. Arlington* (1992) wrote, "School officials must come to the IEP table with an open mind. But this does not mean they should come to the IEP table with a blank mind" (p. 2). School IEP team members can meet and discuss programming or placement decisions before an IEP meeting; however, they must come to the actual IEP meeting ready to discuss and collaborate with other IEP team members. Only at the end of an IEP meeting can final decisions about services and placement be made.

Substantive guidelines. We now present four substantive guidelines that will ensure a legally compliant IEP (figure 6.4). First, following a complete, nondiscriminatory evaluation (discussed in chapter 5), the IEP team must develop accurate and comprehensive PLAAFP statements. One of the most important components of an IEP is the section on PLAAFP. To underscore the importance of PLAAFP statements, the U.S. Supreme Court recently wrote in *Endrew* (2017), "focus on the particular child is at the core of the IDEA [. . .] It is constructed only after careful consideration of the child's present levels of achievement, disability, and potential for growth" (p. 12). Comprehensive and accurate PLAAFP statements establish a baseline level of academic and functional performance. The statements should summarize all aspects of a student's present levels and identify both strengths and needs of the student. Harmon et al. (2020) explored multiple factors to consider when developing a student's PLAAFP such as cognitive and executive functioning, communication, behavior, social skills, emotional, motor skills, adaptive skills, and transition (if applicable).

Based on the student's PLAAFP, the IEP team must develop SMART annual goals and short-term objectives. Individualized goals with sufficient detail, that align with present levels of performance and endorse high expectations, are the core of legally defensible IEPs. It is clear that SMART goals promote more than

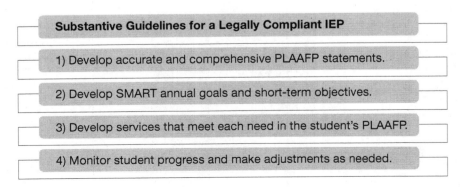

Substantive Guidelines for a Legally Compliant IEP

1) Develop accurate and comprehensive PLAAFP statements.

2) Develop SMART annual goals and short-term objectives.

3) Develop services that meet each need in the student's PLAAFP.

4) Monitor student progress and make adjustments as needed.

Figure 6.4   Substantive Guidelines for a Legally Compliant IEP.

de minimis progress. They also allow the IEP team to make data-based decisions and justify that an IEP is reasonably calculated to confer appropriate progress in light of the student's circumstances.

Now that goals and objectives are drafted, the IEP team must identify and develop special education and related services to address the goals and meet each need in the student's PLAAFP. An IEP team cannot determine services based on availability, nor on cost. Services must be based on the student's academic and functional needs. Also, the supports and services should focus on involvement in the general education curriculum. IDEA regulations (2012) state an IEP must include

> A statement of the special education and related services and supplementary aids and services, based on peer-reviewed research to the extent practicable, to be provided to the child, or on behalf of the child, and a statement of the program modification or supports for school personnel that will be provided to enable the child—(i) To advance appropriately toward attaining the annual goals; (ii) To be involved in and make progress in the general education curriculum [. . .] and to participate in extracurricular and other nonacademic activities; and (iii) To be educated and participate with other children with disabilities and nondisabled children. (34 C.F.R. § 300.39)

Determining a student's placement should only occur after the IEP is developed, avoiding predetermination. The placement decision must be based on the student's individual needs, not resource availability, or a mentality of "this is how and where we educate students with learning disabilities."

Following IEP finalization and implementation, the school must monitor student progress and make adjustments as needed. According to Deno (1992), progress monitoring creates a database regarding a student's progress, allowing the teacher to evaluate the student's success and change the program if needed. Data collection and evaluation allow a school to justify the level of special education services to show an IEP is reasonably calculated to enable the child to make progress appropriate in light of the student's circumstances. Again, the IEP is not a guarantee of success; however, the school must make good-faith efforts to assist the student in making more than de minimis progress. Data-based and data-driven IEPs will show that the student is making progress, or that the IEP team is collecting and analyzing data to adjust special education services as needed.

For both procedural and substantive guidelines, the IEP team must develop, implement, monitor, and adjust the IEP in good faith. Critical to those good-faith efforts are including and collaborating with parents who are essential members of the IEP team. Unforeseen circumstances do occur, and school personnel make mistakes. The courts, however, have been more lenient in denial of FAPE cases when schools can demonstrate that good-faith efforts were made to follow all procedural and substantive requirements.

Circling back to where we began, the IEP is an essential pillar of IDEA. It is the cornerstone of special education, revealed in both a process and product. The IEP is the vehicle that delivers the belief that all students deserve access and accountability in education to improve their quality of life.

Where can I find more information about individualized education programs?

The Center for Parent Resources and Information (**www.parentcenterhub .org**). A parent-friendly resource that provides information about individualized education programs in both English and Spanish. To access this resource visit https://www.parentcenterhub.org/iep/.

IRIS Center (iris.peabody.vanderbilt.edu). A website created by Vanderbilt University that provides modules on developing SMART goals as well as information briefs on common procedural and substantive errors during the IEP process. Find these at https://iris.peabody.vanderbilt.edu/.

What is an IEP? A short video explaining to parents what an IEP is, what is included in an IEP, and who the members of an IEP team are. This video can be found at https://www.youtube.com/watch?v=tGYO9XWhI2Y.

U.S. Department of Education. A guide to individualized education programs by the U.S. Department of Education. This guide can be found at https://www2.ed.gov/parents/needs/speced/iepguide/index.html.

Key Terms

Academically: Related to learning in core subject areas, for example, reading, writing, and math.

Baseline: Data regarding a student's current level of performance.

Functionally: Related to a student's ability in regard to activities of daily living, for example, self-care, daily living, and work-related behaviors.

Good-faith effort: Sincere and honest effort.

Multidisciplinary team: A group of individuals from multiple disciplines (e.g., special education teacher, general education teacher, psychologist, principal) who evaluate a student for special education and collaborate to create an individualized education program.

Progress monitoring: Scheduled data collection to monitor a student's progress toward a goal.

Specially designed instruction (SDI): Adapting the content, methodology, or delivery of instruction to address the unique needs of a student and to ensure access to the general education curriculum.

Discussion Questions

1. What is an IEP? How does it help a student?
2. What is needed for an IEP to be a legally compliant document?
3. How are baselines and progress monitoring used in the IEP process?
4. What are some examples of specially designed instruction?

References

Amanda J. v. Clark County School District, 207 F.3d 877 (9ᵗʰ Cir. 2001).

AquaSource, Inc. v. Wind Dance Farm, Inc., 833 N.E.2d 535, 539 (Ind. App. 2005).

Bateman, B. D. (2017). Individual education programs for children with disabilities. In J. M. Kauffman & D. P. Hallahan. (Eds.), *Handbook of special education* (2nd ed.). (pp. 91-106). Routledge.

Board of Education of the Hendrick Hudson School District v. Rowley, 485 U.S. 176 (1982).

Education of All Handicapped Children Act of 1975, 20 U.S.C. § 1401 (1975).

Endrew F. v. Douglas County School District, 137 S. Ct. 988 (2017).

Every Student Succeeds Act of 2015, Pub. L. No. 114-95, § 4104 (2015).

Federal Register. (2006, August 14). Vol. 71, No. 156.

Goran, L., Harkins Monaco, E. A., Yell, M. L., Shriner, J., & Bateman, D. (2020). Pursuing academic and functional advancement: Goals, services, and measuring progress. *TEACHING Exceptional Children, 52*(5), 333-343. https://doi.org/10.1177/0040059920919924

Harmon, S., Street, M., Bateman, D., & Yell, M. L. (2020). Developing present levels of academic achievement and functional performance statements for IEPs. *Teaching Exceptional Children, 52*(5), 320-332.

Hedin, L., & DeSpain, S. (2018). SMART or not? Writing specific, measurable IEP goals. *Teaching Exceptional Children, 51*(2), 100-110.

IDEA regulations, 34 C.F.R. § 300 (2012).

Individuals with Disabilities Education Act of 2004, 20 U.S.C. § 1400 (2004).

Lake, S. E. (2002). *The top 10 IEP errors: How to avoid them, how to fix them.* LRP Publications.

Lake, S. E. (2007). *Slippery slope: The IEP missteps every team must know—and how to avoid them.* LPR Publications.

No Child Left Behind Act of 2001, P.L. 107-110, 20 U.S.C. § 6319 (2001).

Office of Special Education Programs. (2000). *A guide to the individualized education program.* U.S. Department of Education. Retrieved from https://www2.ed.gov/parents/needs/speced/iepguide/index.html

Prince, A. M. T., Plotner, A. J., & Yell, M. L. (2014). Legal update on postsecondary transition. *Journal of Disability Policy Studies, 25*(1), 41-47.

Smith, S. W. (1990). Individualized education programs (IEPs) in special education—from intent to acquiescence. *Exceptional Children, 57*(1), 6-14.

Yell, M. L. (2019). *The law and special education* (5th ed.). Pearson Education.

Yell, M. L., Katsiyannais, A., Ennis, R. P., & Losinski, M. (2013). Avoiding procedural errors in IEP development. *Focus on Exceptional Children, 46*(1), 31-40.

Yell, M. L., Katsiyannis, A., Ennis, R. P., Losinski, M., & Bateman, D. (2020). Making legally sound placement decisions. *Teaching Exceptional Children, 52*(5), 291-303. https://doi.org/10.1177/0040059920906537

Zirkel, P. A., & Hetrick, A. (2017). Which procedural parts of the IEP process are the most judicially vulnerable? *Exceptional Children, 83*(2), 219–235. https://doi.org/10.1177/0014402916651849

CHAPTER 7

Least Restrictive Environment

> *When students with disabilities are meaningfully included in the least restrictive environment for their unique needs, they are welcomed into a wider school community and gain access to friendships, grade-level academic content, and peer role models.*
>
> *Emily Hanaway*
> *Special Education Teacher in Texas*

When the U.S. Supreme Court ruled in *Brown v. Board of Education* (1954) that racial segregation was unconstitutional in public schools, disability advocates applied the court's rationale to students with disabilities. In the 1950s and 1960s, the few students with disabilities who did receive a public education were often relegated to poor facilities that were under-resourced, understaffed, and segregated from nondisabled children (Martin, 2013). Disability advocates cited the "separate is never equal" doctrine of *Brown v. Board of Education* and urged Congress to adopt measures that would require school districts to educate students with disabilities alongside their nondisabled peers (Yell & Christle, 2017). As the Education of All Handicapped Children Act (EAHCA) of 1975 was being drafted, an amendment was added by Senator Robert Stafford of Vermont to prevent the educational segregation of students with disabilities. This amendment was added to the final piece of legislation and became known as the least restrictive environment (LRE) mandate. The Individuals with Disabilities Education Act (IDEA) of 2004 maintains the LRE mandate, which is a fundamental concept in protecting the rights of students with disabilities. In this chapter we will discuss the fourth pillar of special education, LRE (figure 7.1), and answer these essential questions:

1. What is meant by least restrictive environment?
2. How does least restrictive environment relate to free appropriate public education?

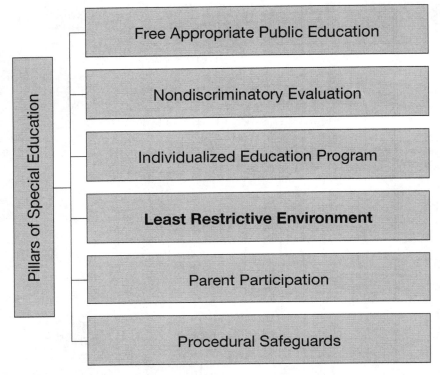

Figure 7.1   Least Restrictive Environment Is the Fourth Pillar of Special Education.

3. What regulations and court cases have defined least restrictive environment?
4. How do I ensure least restrictive environment?
5. Where can I find more information about least restrictive environment?

What is meant by least restrictive environment?

Basically, the LRE mandate requires that students with disabilities be educated in settings alongside students without disabilities, when appropriate. IDEA (2004) specifically states:

> To the maximum extent appropriate, children with disabilities, including children in public or private institutions or other care facilities, are educated with children who are not disabled, and that special classes, separate schooling, or other removal of children with disabilities from the regular educational environment occurs only when the nature or severity of the disability is such that education in regular classes with the use of supplementary aids and services cannot be achieved.

"Restrictiveness" refers to the degree to which a student has proximity to, and communication with, nondisabled peers (Champagne, 1993). Based on this definition of restrictiveness, the general education environment is the least restrictive setting because it allows for maximum proximity and communication with nondisabled peers. **Inclusion** and **mainstreaming** are sometimes used in exchange for LRE; however, they do not mean the same thing as LRE.

"Inclusion" and "mainstreaming" (now an outdated term) refer to a general philosophy that students with disabilities should spend the majority or all of their time in the general education environment. There are educational philosophies about the benefits of a particular setting. Inclusion may be the LRE for some students with disabilities, but it may not be the LRE for other students with disabilities. It is important to remember that a student's LRE is not just about a setting but also about special education services. The specific determination of a student's LRE revolves around whether an educational program and setting is appropriate. Similarly to the pillar of free appropriate public education (FAPE), we again encounter the subjective word "appropriate." As we will learn by answering the next essential question, the appropriateness of a student's LRE is directly tied to the appropriateness of a student's FAPE.

How does least restrictive environment relate to free appropriate public education?

When attempting to clarify the level of educational benefit schools must provide to satisfy the appropriateness of a student's FAPE, the Supreme Court struck a middle ground. The lower standard of de minimis was rejected, as well as the higher standard established by some district courts. As we discussed in chapter 4, the Supreme Court stated, "to meet the substantive obligation under IDEA, a school must offer an IEP reasonably calculated to enable a child to make progress appropriate in light of the child's circumstances" (*Endrew F. v. Douglas County School District*, 2017). The Supreme Court clarified that appropriate progress, therefore, is highly individualized dependent on a student's circumstances. A student's LRE, therefore, is also highly individualized and dependent on their circumstances.

Although the LRE mandate requires schools to place students in settings that are least restrictive (i.e., alongside their nondisabled peers), that may not be the most appropriate setting for a student to receive FAPE. The two special education pillars of LRE and FAPE, therefore, are interconnected yet sometimes in conflict. Given that special education is about the educational progress of a student, the appropriateness of that education (i.e., FAPE) **supersedes** the restrictiveness of an environment (i.e., LRE).

In other words, schools must strive to educate students with disabilities in less restrictive settings; however, the appropriateness of that setting can only be determined by whether the student can make appropriate educational progress in light of their circumstances.

Knowing that the general education classroom may not be the most appropriate setting for all students with disabilities, a **continuum of placements** was established in IDEA (2004; see figure 7.2).

The purpose of the continuum was for schools to have options to choose from when determining the most appropriate LRE for a student. Because restrictiveness is determined by degree of proximity and communication with

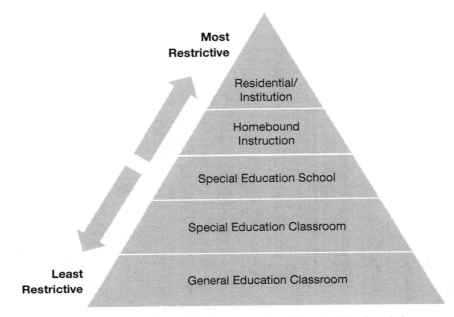

**Most
Restrictive**

Residential/
Institution

Homebound
Instruction

Special Education School

Special Education Classroom

**Least
Restrictive**   General Education Classroom

Figure 7.2 Continuum of Placements from Least Restrictive to Most Restrictive.

nondisabled peers, the least restrictive environment is the general education classroom; however, that is not always the most appropriate environment. Some students may require more individualized instruction or a modified curriculum. These students may benefit from educational services that can be better provided in a separate classroom. Other students with severe disabilities may be best educated in a separate school or hospital setting where intensive medical needs can be addressed. There are a multitude of placement and service options between the least restrictive and most restrictive environments. Because there is no clear definition of what is or is not a student's LRE, there have been many due process hearings on the tension between LRE and FAPE.

What regulations and court cases have defined least restrictive environment?

Although IDEA (2004) clearly suggests that the general education setting is the least restrictive environment, the LRE for each student should be determined by the professional judgment of the individual education program (IEP) team (Palley, 2009). The IEP team determines which placement along the continuum is least restrictive while also most appropriate. If the general education setting cannot provide appropriate educational benefit in light of the student's circumstances, a more restrictive placement is necessary to provide educational benefit.

Disagreements between parents and schools over placement decisions have resulted in a number of court cases. The U.S. Supreme Court has not heard a case interpreting the LRE mandate. Therefore, varying U.S. Circuit Courts of Appeals rulings are the highest authority to provide guidance. Four tests have been developed and used by circuit courts to determine a school's compliance with the LRE mandate (see table 7.1). The following section will examine these cases and tests.

The Roncker Test (Sixth and Eighth Circuits). One of the first court cases to deal with LRE was *Roncker v. Walter* (1983). Neil Roncker was a nine-year-old student with a moderate intellectual disability. Neil's school believed the most appropriate placement for him was a special school for children with disabilities. His parents disagreed and stated that the best placement for Neil would be in the general education classroom with supports and services. They believed Neil would benefit from greater integration and contact with his nondisabled

TABLE 7.1 Circuit Court Tests When Determining Least Restrictive Environment

The Roncker Test	1. Can the educational services that make a more restrictive placement appropriate be feasibly provided in a less restrictive placement? 2. If so, the placement in the more restrictive setting is inappropriate.
The Daniel Test	1. Can education in the general education classroom with supplementary aids and services be achieved satisfactorily? 2. If a student is placed in a more restrictive setting, is the student integrated to the maximum extent appropriate?
The Rachel Test	Factors to consider when determining LRE placement: 1. The educational benefits of the general education classroom with supplementary aids and services as compared with the educational benefits of the special classroom. 2. The nonacademic benefits of the interaction with students without disabilities. 3. The effect of the student's presence on the teacher and on other students in the classroom. 4. The cost of inclusion.
The DeVries Test	Inclusion is not required when: 1. A student with a disability would not receive educational benefit from inclusion in a general education class. 2. Any marginal benefit from inclusion would be significantly outweighed by benefits that could feasibly be obtained only in a separate instructional setting. 3. The student is a disruptive force in the general education classroom.

peers. After a U.S. District Court ruled in favor of the school, the Roncker family appealed to the U.S. Court of Appeals for the Sixth Circuit.

The Sixth Circuit Court reinforced that the congressional intent of the LRE mandate was for the general educational setting, but that it is not always appropriate in every case. The Roncker portability test was developed to help schools and courts distinguish between the benefits of segregated special education services and inclusion in the general education setting. In essence, the court claimed that if a more restrictive environment is deemed appropriate, the school should determine whether the services that make that placement appropriate could feasibly be provided in a less restrictive setting. If they can, then placement in a more restrictive setting is inappropriate under IDEA (2004; *Roncker v. Walter*, 1983). This standard of review applies to the Sixth Circuit Court of Appeals (Kentucky, Michigan, Ohio, Tennessee). Shortly after, the U.S. Court of Appeals for the Eighth Circuit adopted the Roncker test to analyze the issue of LRE and inclusion. The Eighth Circuit is Arkansas, Iowa, Missouri, Minnesota, Nebraska, North Dakota, and South Dakota.

The Daniel R. R. Test (Second, Third, Fifth, Tenth, and Eleventh Circuits). *Daniel R. R. v. State Board of Education* (1989) is a seminal court case about LRE (Yell, 2019). The case was heard by the Fifth Circuit Court, but the ruling had persuasive authority for several other circuit courts. Daniel was a six-year-old child with Downs syndrome enrolled in a Texas school district. At his parents' request, Daniel attended a general education prekindergarten class for half the day and a special education class for the other half. Shortly after the school year started, Daniel's teacher informed the school that Daniel was not mastering any of the early childhood skills being taught, rarely participated in classroom activities, and required an extensive amount of individual attention and instruction. The school decided that the prekindergarten classroom was not an appropriate setting for Daniel and placed him exclusively in the special education class. Daniel's parents disagreed with the placement and requested a **due process hearing.**

The hearing officer and federal district court both agreed with the school that Daniel was receiving little educational benefit in the prekindergarten classroom and that his needs could be met more appropriately in a special education class. Daniel's parents appealed to the Fifth Circuit Court.

The Fifth Circuit Court also ruled in favor of the school that a more restrictive environment was appropriate for Daniel to receive educational benefit. The court emphasized that the determination of appropriate educational methods is best handled by local school professionals. Because an appropriate education is more important than a least restrictive education, when FAPE and LRE are in conflict, the LRE mandate becomes secondary to the FAPE provision (*Daniel R. R. v. State Board of Education*, 1989).

The Fifth Circuit Court dismissed the Roncker Test of the Sixth Circuit Court as too intrusive in the educational choices of local school districts and developed its own two-part test. The Daniel R. R. Test allows schools to determine if they are complying with the LRE mandate by asking: (1) can education in the general education classroom with **supplementary aids and services** be achieved satisfactorily?

To answer this question, schools must decide if the general education classroom can provide educational benefit for the student. Also, the included student must not negatively affect the education of classroom peers. The Fifth Circuit Court realized that Daniel's needs were not being met in the general education classroom and that he was negatively impacting the ability of his teacher to attend to and instruct other students. The second part of the Daniel Test is: (2) if a student is placed in a more restrictive setting, is the student integrated to the maximum extent appropriate? For a student who is placed in more restrictive settings to obtain an appropriate education, that student must be included and integrated with their nondisabled peers to the greatest extent possible, for example, inclusion during lunch, recess, and nonacademic classes. If a school satisfies both parts of the Daniel R. R. Test, then their obligation under IDEA to provide appropriate education in a student's LRE is met.

The Daniel R. R. test applies in the Fifth Circuit (Louisiana, Mississippi, and Texas), and was adopted by the Second Circuit (New York, Vermont, Connecticut), the Third Circuit (Pennsylvania, New Jersey, Delaware), the Tenth Circuit (Wyoming, Utah, Colorado, Kansas, New Mexico, Oklahoma), and the Eleventh Circuit (Alabama, Georgia, Florida).

The Rachel H. Test (Ninth Circuit). In *Sacramento City Unified School District Board of Education v. Rachel H.* (1994), the Ninth Circuit Court built upon the Roncker and Daniel R. R. Tests to establish a four-part test to determine compliance with the LRE mandate. Rachel Holland was an eleven-year-old girl with a moderate intellectual disability. After attending special education programs for a number of years, Rachel's parents wanted her placed in a general education classroom with supplementary aids and services for the entire school day. The school suggested that Rachel's disability was too severe to benefit from the general education classroom. School personnel recommended placing her in a special education class for academic subjects but in a general education class for nonacademic subjects. The parents disagreed and requested a due process hearing. The case ended up in the Ninth Circuit Court where the judges considered four factors in making their decision.

The first factor considers the educational benefit of the general education classroom with supplementary aids and services versus the educational benefit of a more restrictive setting. In this case, the court found the district did not present evidence that the educational benefit for Rachel in a special education classroom was greater than the educational benefit in a general education classroom.

The second factor considers the nonacademic benefits (e.g., social interaction with nondisabled peers) of the general education classroom versus a more restrictive setting. After hearing testimony from the case, the court decided Rachel was benefiting from social interactions with her peers. Therefore, the general education classroom was providing more nonacademic benefits than a special education classroom.

The third factor considers the effect of the presence of a student on the teacher and other students in the classroom. If a student is greatly disruptive or requires individual teacher attention subtracting from the educational benefit of other students, then a more restrictive setting might be appropriate. Both parties in this case agreed that Rachel was neither disruptive nor distracting. The court also found that she did not require extensive individual instruction from her teacher that interfered with the education of other students.

The fourth factor considers the cost of placement in the general education classroom. The school did not convince the court that Rachel's placement in the general education classroom with supplementary aids and services was far more expensive than placement in a special education classroom. Thus, cost was not a barrier to educating Rachel in the general education classroom. After considering all four factors, the Ninth Circuit Court ruled in favor of Rachel and her parents that her appropriate placement was in the general education classroom with supplementary aids and services.

The *Rachel H.* test is the legal authority for the Ninth Circuit, which covers Alaska, Arizona, California, Hawaii, Idaho, Montana, Nevada, Oregon, and Washington.

The DeVries Test (Fourth Circuit). In 1989, the Fourth Circuit Court took a slightly different approach in *DeVries v. Fairfax County School Board* by applying a three-part test to determine when the general education classroom is *not* appropriate. Michael DeVries was a seventeen-year-old high school student with autism. His IEP team determined that his most appropriate placement would be at a vocational school that was miles away from his home school. Michael's parents did not agree with the vocational school placement and wanted him to attend his neighborhood school, so they requested a due process hearing.

The Fourth Circuit Court heard the case and ruled in favor of the lower courts' rulings that Michael's appropriate placement was in the vocational school. The court looked at Michael's individual circumstances and concluded inclusion was not an appropriate placement because (a) he would not receive educational benefit in a general education classroom; (b) any social benefit that inclusion with his nondisabled peers might provide was outweighed by the educational benefit he would receive at the vocational school; and (c) his behaviors were disruptive.

The DeVries test is the legal authority for the U.S. Court of Appeals for the Fourth Circuit (Maryland, North Carolina, South Carolina, Virginia, West Virginia).

Common factors between circuit courts. Four separate tests have controlling authority over states to determine compliance with the LRE mandate of IDEA. Five common factors, however, have emerged from the various court cases. Figure 7.3 lists each factor.

First, the courts agree that IDEA clearly identifies the general education classroom as the preferred setting for students with disabilities. The courts have consistently reinforced that the congressional intent of the law was for students with disabilities to be educated alongside their nondisabled peers to the maximum extent appropriate.

Second, the courts agree that educational benefit supersedes social benefit. Social interaction with nondisabled peers is important and the courts have

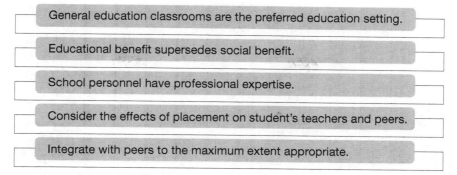

General education classrooms are the preferred education setting.

Educational benefit supersedes social benefit.

School personnel have professional expertise.

Consider the effects of placement on student's teachers and peers.

Integrate with peers to the maximum extent appropriate.

Figure 7.3 Common Factors from Court Cases When Determining Least Restrictive Environment.

stated so. However, the LRE mandate to include students with disabilities in the general education classroom is secondary to the provision of providing an appropriate education.

Third, the courts are reluctant to question the professional judgment of educators as to what constitutes appropriate educational services. The IEP team consists of education professionals who have evaluated the student and understand their educational needs and the instructional services required to meet those needs. Substantial authority by the courts, therefore, has been deferred to school personnel for determining the appropriate placement in which a student will benefit educationally.

Fourth, schools should consider the effects that inclusion of a student with a disability will have on the teacher and other students in the classroom. Schools are not helpless when a student with a disability demonstrates disruptive and aggressive behaviors. The safety and educational well-being of other students must be considered when determining appropriate placement. If supplementary aids and services cannot reduce disruptive behaviors, or individual instruction requires too much teacher attention, then the general education classroom is likely not the student's LRE.

Lastly, if a more restricted environment is required, schools must integrate students with disabilities with their nondisabled peers to the maximum extent appropriate. The courts have attempted to strike a balance between the realities of providing appropriate educational services and the doctrine of *Brown v. Board of Education* (1954) that separate is never equal. Although the ideal is for every student to be educated in the general education setting with supplementary aids and services, some students require more intensive interventions that can only be provided in a more restrictive environment.

How do I ensure least restrictive environment?

Most often, the IEP team will determine a student's LRE placement. This decision must be revisited, and revised if needed, at least annually. It is the team's responsibility to determine the placement along the continuum that is least restrictive while also most appropriate educationally. When making this determination, there are some things an IEP team should do and not do to ensure a student's appropriate LRE is decided (see figure 7.4).

It is important for an IEP team to comprehensively understand a student's educational needs prior to determining their LRE placement. A student's

What To Do

- Conduct a comprehensive evaluation to determine the student's educational needs

- Develop an individualized educational program with supplemental aids and services, related services, and program modifications that provide educational benefit to the student.

- Meaningfully involve parents or guardians in the determination of placement

- Start placement discussion at the general education classroom to determine if supplementary aids and services can confer appropriate educational benefit.

- If the general education classroom is not appropriate, move down the continuum of placements one setting at a time until an appropriate placement is determined.

- Once placement is determined, ask if additional opportunities exist for integration with peers.

What Not To Do

- Make placement decision on factors unrelated to the student's educational needs.

- Predetermine the student's placement prior to understanding their educational needs.

- Make placement decision because "that's the way it has been done."

- Place student in setting because other options are not available.

- Make a placement decision based on cost of services unless choosing between multiple options that provide equal educational benefit.

- Finalize the student's placement prior to the IEP meeting.

Figure 7.4 What to Do and What Not to Do to Ensure Appropriate LRE.

LRE placement is where those educational needs can be best met while also included with nondisabled peers to the greatest extent possible. Placement decisions that are based on factors unrelated to a student's educational needs, for example, disability category, availability of services, or administrative convenience, are not valid reasons. Placing a student in a more restrictive environment (e.g., a **life skills classroom**) because "that's where students with intellectual disabilities" are taught is also not an acceptable LRE justification.

An IEP team must first collaborate with a student's parents and develop an individualized education program with goals. Then, the team can determine LRE placement. The team should always start by asking, is the general education classroom with supplementary aids and services an appropriate setting for the student to make educational progress? If the team decides that the general education classroom is not appropriate, then the next restrictive environment down the continuum of placements should be considered. For example, can the student make appropriate progress in a **resource room** for a limited amount of time each week or day? Based on the student's educational needs, the team should work down the continuum until a placement is determined that is most appropriate for the student's individual needs.

Lastly, if the final LRE determination is in a setting more restrictive than the general education classroom, the IEP team must ask if additional opportunities exist throughout the school day for the student to be included in activities with nondisabled peers. IDEA is clear that the general education classroom with supplementary aids and services is the preferred educational setting for students with disabilities. However, a student's individual needs must be the primary factor when deciding placement. Although an appropriate education takes priority over a restrictive education, the IEP team must remember that separate is never equal. Including and educating students with disabilities alongside their nondisabled peers, to the maximum extent appropriate, is the only way to ensure the LRE mandate of IDEA is fulfilled.

Where can I find more information about least restrictive environment?

Center for Parent Information and Resources (www.parentcenterhub.org). A parent-friendly resource that provides information about least restrictive environment in both English and Spanish. To access this resource visit https://www.parentcenterhub.org/placement-lre/.

U.S. Department of Education—IDEA. Access the statutory section in IDEA about LRE requirements at https://sites.ed.gov/idea/regs/b/b/300.114.

IDEA Basics: (LRE) Least Restrictive Environment. In this video, a special education advocate and special education attorney discuss LRE. The short video presents and discusses important concepts of LRE that parents of children with disabilities should know. Visit https://www.youtube.com/watch?v=I7HFRF8y288.

State-Specific LRE Information. For state-specific LRE information, Google your state's education department and "least restrictive environment." Each state will have guidance documents and other important information pertaining to state-specific LRE requirement.

Key Terms

Continuum of placements: The range of educational placement settings where a student's IEP can be implemented from least restrictive (general education classroom) to most restrictive (residential hospital/institution).

Due process hearing: Similar to a courtroom trial where both sides of a dispute can present evidence, call witnesses, and make legal arguments. A hearing officer or judge oversees the trial and makes a judgment.

Inclusion: An educational philosophy that students with a disability should be educated alongside their nondisabled peers with supports and services.

Life skills classroom: A special education classroom for students with more severe disabilities. A modified curriculum focuses on functional, adaptive, social, and academic skills specific to students' individual needs.

Mainstreaming: An outdated term representing an educational philosophy that students with disabilities should spend time with their nondisabled peers for a portion of the day (i.e., recess, nonacademic classes, lunch).

Resource room: A special education classroom for students with less severe disabilities. Specialized instruction and academic remediation are provided for students' individual needs. Students with disabilities attend a resource room for only part of the school day or a few times a week.

Supersedes: Takes the place of what was previously in authority; a new priority.

Supplementary aids and services: Aids, services, and other supports that are provided in general education classes, other education-related settings, and extracurricular and nonacademic settings, and that enable students with disabilities to be educated with nondisabled students to the maximum extent appropriate.

Discussion Questions

1. Why are LRE and FAPE sometimes in conflict with one another?

2. Do you agree that FAPE should be prioritized above LRE?

3. What factors must be considered when determining LRE?

4. Why might an LRE decision cause conflict between parents and the school?

5. What supports can be provided so that a student with a disability can remain in a general education setting?

References

Brown v. Board of Education, 347 U.S. 483 (1954).

Champagne, J. F. (1993). Decisions in sequence: How to make placements in the least restrictive environment. *EdLaw Briefing Paper, 9&10*, 1-16.

Daniel R. R. v. State Board of Education, 874 F.2d 1036 (5th Cir. 1989).

DeVries v. Fairfax County School Board, 853 F.2d 264 (4th Cir. 1989).

Education of All Handicapped Children Act of 1975, 20 U.S.C. § 1401.

Endrew F. v. Douglas County School District, 137 S. Ct. 988 (2017).

Individuals with Disabilities Education Act of 2004, 20 U.S.C. § 1400.

Martin, E. (2013). *Breakthrough: Federal special education legislation: 1965-1981*. Bardolf & Company.

Palley, E. (2009). Civil rights for people with disabilities: Obstacles related to the least restrictive environment mandate. *Journal of Social Work in Disability and Rehabilitation, 8*, 37-55.

Roncker v. Walter, 700 F.2d 1058 (6th Cir. 1983).

Sacramento City Unified School District Board of Education v. Rachel H., 14 F.3d 1398 (9th Cir. 1994).

Yell, M. L. (2019). *The law and special education* (5th ed.). Pearson Education.

Yell, M. L, & Christle, C. A. (2017). The foundation of inclusion in federal legislation and litigation. In C. M. Curran & A. J. Petersen (Eds.) *The handbook of research on classroom diversity and inclusive education practice* (pp. 27-74). IGI Global.

CHAPTER 8

Parent Participation

> *Parents are equal members of the IEP team, and their input, ideas, and suggestions should be treated with the same consideration and respect that is given to other professionals within the team.*
>
> *Sasha Anderson*
> *Special Education Teacher in Idaho*

P arents play a vital role as team members in the development and monitoring of their child's individualized education program (IEP). Although educational professionals on the IEP team (i.e., school principal, school psychologist, special education teacher) are responsible for procedural and substantive requirements, the Individuals with Disabilities Education Act (IDEA) has specific guidelines that schools must follow to ensure parent participation in all aspects of their child's special education services. As discussed in chapter 6, an IEP is a legal contract between a school and the parents of child with a disability. Parents must be involved in the development of that legal contract and included in any changes that take place. Much of the litigation relating to parent participation comes down to problems with communication. Therefore, special education teachers must follow procedural guidelines outlined in IDEA and implement effective communication strategies to guarantee parent participation. In this chapter, we will discuss the fifth pillar of special education, parent participation (figure 8.1), and answer these essential questions:

1. What is parent participation?
2. How does parent participation relate to free appropriate public education?
3. What regulations and court cases have defined parent participation?
4. How do I ensure parent participation?
5. Where can I find more information about parent participation?

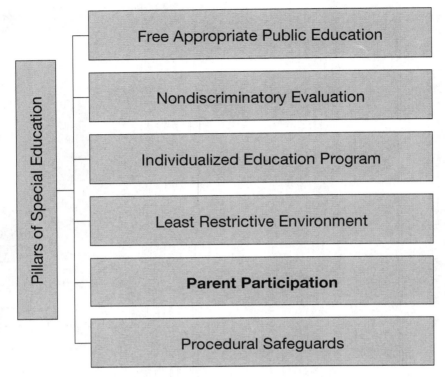

Figure 8.1 Parent Participation Is the Fifth Pillar of Special Education.

What is parent participation?

Before we discuss parent participation, we need to clarify what may seem simple, but in the end, is fairly complex: who is a parent? Throughout this chapter we will use the term "parent" but as you will see, under IDEA the term "parent" can mean many things, such as:

- A biological or adoptive parent of a child.
- A foster parent, unless state law, regulations, or contractual obligations with a state or local entity prohibit a foster parent from acting as a parent.
- A guardian generally authorized to act as the child's parent or authorized to make educational decisions for the child (but not the state if the child is a ward of the state).
- An individual acting in the place of a biological or adoptive parent (including a grandparent, stepparent, or another relative) with whom the child lives or an individual who is legally responsible for the child's welfare.
- A surrogate parent who has been appointed in accordance with the law.
- Except in the case of foster parents, when a biological or adoptive parent attempts to act as the parent, and more than one party is qualified to act as a parent, the biological or adoptive parent is presumed to be the parent

unless they do not have the authority to make educational decisions for the child.

- Divorced parents: if a court order or agreement identifies a specific person to act as the "parent" of a child or to make educational decisions on behalf of a child, then such person shall be determined to be the parent.

Parents are essential partners in special education and legally required members of IEP teams. Based on previous chapters, we know that the primary goal of IDEA is to provide a free appropriate public education (FAPE) in the least restrictive environment (LRE) for all eligible students with disabilities. Congress recognized that school districts maintained a lot of power in the process of identifying eligibility and developing IEPs due to school personnel's **professional expertise.**

Members of the IEP team such as teachers, school psychologists, and principals would likely have more knowledge on procedural and substantive components of IDEA based on their training. In order for parents to fully participate and advocate for their children in the IDEA process, Congress included significant and numerous parental rights in the statute. Table 8.1 outlines eight major legal entitlements under IDEA for parents to participate in the IEP process of their child.

In essence, the eight entitlements under IDEA were established to afford parents the opportunity to (a) access and evaluate school-collected data on their child, (b) participate in decision-making affecting their child's education as an

---

TABLE 8.1   Eight Major Legal Rights Allowing Parents to Participate in the IEP Process

1. The right of parents to receive a complete explanation of all the procedural safeguards available under IDEA and the procedures in the state for presenting complaints.
2. Confidentiality and the right of parents to inspect and review the educational records of their child.
3. The right of parents to participate in meetings related to the identification, evaluation, and placement of their child.
4. The right of parents to obtain an independent educational evaluation of their child.
5. The right of parents to receive "prior written notice" on matters relating to the identification, evaluation, or placement of their child.
6. The right of parents to give or deny their consent before the school may take certain actions with respect to their child.
7. The right of parents to disagree with decisions made by the school district.
8. The right of parents to use IDEA mechanisms for resolving disputes, including the right to appeal determinations.

Source. Center for Parent Information and Resources (2017).

informed member, and (c) understand their legal rights and the procedures to challenge a school's decision in case of disagreement. As we will now explore, these three legal components of parent participation directly relate to the next essential question.

How does parent participation relate to free appropriate public education?

It is evident that IDEA is comprised of procedural and substantive requirements. The relation between parent participation and FAPE is no different. There are procedural requirements special education teachers must follow to ensure FAPE is procedurally provided, as well as substantive requirements to guarantee an appropriate education.

Procedural requirements of parent participation. The first procedural step to parent participation is notification. Schools must take steps to ensure one or both parents are present at the IEP meeting. Therefore, parents must be given sufficient notice of the IEP development meeting so that they can attend. How much notice do parents need before a meeting? The federal regulation does not mention specific timelines in connection with scheduling IEP meetings. However, districts must notify parents of the IEP meeting early enough in advance of the meeting to ensure they will have an opportunity to attend. The written notice to parents must contain the purpose of the meeting, time and location, and persons to be in attendance. The school must work with the parents to schedule a meeting at a mutually agreeable time. The school does not have to agree with a parent's demanded time and date; however, the district must make good-faith efforts to mutually agree on scheduling (Yell, 2019). If a parent cannot be contacted to attend the IEP meeting, a school has an obligation to develop the IEP and provide FAPE. The school must have a documented record of multiple attempts to contact the parent and arrange a meeting. Examples of documentation may include:

- Records of telephone calls made or attempted and the results of those calls.
- Copies of correspondence sent to the parents and any responses received.
- Records of visits made to the parent's home or place of employment and the results of those visits.

The second procedural step to parent participation is access to records and data. Whether a meeting is for an initial evaluation and eligibility determination, or an IEP annual review, parents have the right to be given their child's performance data. Furthermore, the information provided must be explained to parents in a logical manner so that they can participate in decision-making as informed members. Parents likely do not have the professional training to interpret and analyze assessment data. Therefore, efforts must be made by the IEP team to explain assessment results and answer any clarification questions parents may have.

Before an IEP meeting, parents must be presented with a draft IEP, not a completed (i.e., finalized) document. In order to participate in an IEP meeting, parents need to access the draft IEP so that they can read the document and prepare to engage in a meaningful way. Parent participation is meaningless if parents do not understand what is going on. Federal regulations state schools must take whatever action is necessary to ensure parents understand the proceedings of the IEP meeting, including arranging for an interpreter for parents whose native language is other than English. If English is not the parents' first language, school districts may be required to provide an interpreter. If an in-person English interpreter is not available, most school districts have a call-in service where an interpreter can provide services via telephone.

Parents who have a disability, or are perceived to have a disability, require schools to take whatever action is necessary to ensure the parent understands the proceedings at the IEP meeting. Actions could include recording the meeting; providing an interpreter for someone who is deaf/hard of hearing or a guide for someone who requires help getting into the building; or providing materials in Braille or large print. The important part is to do what it takes to ensure the parent can fully participate.

The third step to procedural parent participation is informing parents of their legal rights by providing procedural safeguards. Procedural safeguards are so important they are considered the sixth pillar of special education. We will discuss procedural safeguards in detail in chapter 9.

Substantive requirements of parent participation. The procedural requirements of parent participation are intended for parents to become knowledgeable about their child's education and attend IEP meetings. The substantive requirements of parent participation are to ensure **meaningful** participation.

Throughout history, parents have been strong advocates for the betterment of their children's education. Parents know their children and want what is best for them. In fact, special education would not be what it is today without parental advocacy (see chapter 2). Congress did not want parents to be passive members of an IEP team; Congress wanted parents to participate meaningfully, as equal members. When IDEA was first passed in 1975, Congress wrote,

> Almost 30 years of research and experience has demonstrated that the education of children with disabilities can be made more effective by—strengthening the role and responsibility of parents and ensuring families [. . .] have meaningful opportunities to participate in the education of their children at school and at home. (IDEA, 2004)

IEP meetings are the best opportunity for parents to participate in the development of an appropriate education for their child. As the IEP team makes decisions about LRE placement, annual goals, levels of support, and related services, parents must be genuinely included in the discussions. Their opinions and suggestions should be solicited and considered. Parent participation does not mean, however, that parents have absolute authority over placement, program, and related services. Parents are not superior members of an IEP team; rather, they are equal partners. Anyone who is tasked with leading an IEP meeting should be aware that active listening skills, negotiation, and compromise will be needed to agree on a final IEP. We present several parent participation strategies for a successful IEP meeting at the end of this chapter.

School district IEP team members must avoid **predetermination** of a student's program or placement. Predetermination is when a finalized IEP is presented at an IEP meeting, or the school district already decides a student's placement or special education services before parental participation. Unilaterally determining a student's placement and program prior to the actual IEP meeting denies parents meaningful participation in the IEP process and is likely a violation of FAPE (Yell, 2019). School districts may prepare a draft IEP to discuss at an IEP meeting; however, schools must be willing to consider parental input and incorporate suggestions before finalizing the IEP. School districts should avoid statements that could be interpreted as predetermination, such as "in our school, all students diagnosed with a learning disability receive forty-five minutes of resource room instruction a day." Such statements do not satisfy the individualized component of special education services, nor do they allow parents to recommend other placements or services.

What regulations and court cases have defined parent participation?

The executive branch and the judicial branch have both emphasized the importance of parent participation. Although the substantive requirement of meaningful participation is subjective, courts have ruled very clearly on the procedural requirements.

Doug C. v. Hawaii (2013). Doug C. was the father of Spencer, an eighteen-year-old student with autism. Ever since fifth grade, Spencer had been placed in a private special education school. Spencer's IEP meeting was supposed to take place in October, but Doug was unable to attend. The school district proposed a meeting in early November, which Doug could also not attend. Finally, a date was set for November 9; however, on the day of the proposed meeting, Doug requested the IEP meeting be rescheduled because he was sick. Knowing that Spencer's annual IEP review deadline was November 13, the school proposed meeting either November 10 or 11. The school even proposed conducting the meeting via telephone so Doug could attend if he was not feeling well enough to attend in person. Doug stated he wanted to be physically present and could not attend on the 10th or 11th. The special education coordinator decided to proceed with the November 9 meeting even though the parent would not be in attendance.

During the annual IEP meeting, the school decided to change Spencer's placement from the private school to a workplace readiness program at a public high school. The school sent the revised IEP to Doug and set up a follow-up meeting in December. Doug rejected the IEP because he did not participate in its development and did not agree with his son's change in placement. The school did not change their original decision to place Spencer in a new setting. Doug filed a due process hearing alleging that the school district's failure to ensure his participation in the IEP meeting had resulted in a denial of FAPE for his son (Yell et al., 2015).

Doug C. v. Hawaii (2013) was ultimately decided at the Ninth Circuit Court of Appeals. The court ruled in favor of Doug C. and noted in the majority opinion that the school district's efforts to include the parent in the IEP meeting were not sufficient. Even though the school district was concerned with missing Spencer's annual review deadline (a procedural violation of IDEA), the court found that parental participation should take priority over strict adherence to any review timelines. The school district also argued that Doug's repeated cancellations disrupted other IEP team member's schedules, and that therefore a meeting without his presence was warranted. The court also rejected this argument, stating, "The attendance of Doug C., Spencer's parent, must take priority over other members' attendance" (*Doug C. v. Hawaii*, 2013, p. 1,048). Lastly, the school district's argument that a follow-up meeting was held in December to review the IEP was deemed an inappropriate replacement for participation in the development of the IEP. Simply holding a follow-up IEP meeting does not remedy a district's decision to proceed with an IEP meeting without the parent because parental participation is expected in the development of the IEP (Yell et al., 2015).

Amanda J. v. Clark County School District (2001). Amanda was a three-year-old child with perceived delays in communication and daily living skills. She was evaluated by the Clark County School District in Nevada and diagnosed with a developmental delay. When Amanda's mother requested access to her daughter's evaluation records from the district psychologist, she never received them. Amanda started receiving special education services for her diagnosed developmental delay, but, shortly after, moved to California. After arriving in California, Amanda was reevaluated and diagnosed with autism. During the review of educational records for Amanda's evaluation in California, her mother saw for the first time that the Clark County School District in Nevada discussed a possible autism diagnosis. Amanda's mother filed a due process hearing against the Clark County School District, claiming her daughter was denied FAPE from the misdiagnosis of a developmental delay.

Amanda J. v. Clark County School District (2001) was eventually decided by the Ninth Circuit Court of Appeals in favor of Amanda and her family. The court ruled that IDEA was violated, and FAPE denied, because the school district failed to disclose all records to the family which limited their ability to participate as equal members of the IEP team. Had Amanda's mother seen the evaluation documents, perhaps she would have questioned the diagnosis of developmental delay over autism. Failing to provide the evaluation documents was a procedural violation which resulted in a substantive violation. The *Amanda J.* ruling is significant because it reinforces the importance of providing parents with all relevant documents and data so that they can participate as informed members of the IEP team.

How do I ensure parent participation?

A key concept to consider when ensuring parental participation is the idea of **good faith**. Good-faith effort was introduced in chapter 6 and is applicable across many components of special education. Special education teachers must make good-faith efforts to meaningfully include parents. With regard to scheduling

IEP meetings, figure 8.2 provides some best practice strategies. The IEP meeting coordinator should provide date and time options for parents to consider, and all communication between school and parent should be documented.

If face-to-face meetings are inconvenient or impossible, for example, during COVID-19 pandemic restrictions, alternative meeting formats can provide parents an opportunity to participate and to be fully aware of the program and placement for their child. Some important points to consider when setting up alternative meeting formats are:

- Use the parents' preferred means of communication: phone, Skype, Zoom, FaceTime, or others.
- Test the method of communication prior to the meeting.
- Have a backup plan if there is a problem during the meeting.
- Make sure there is a clearly marked draft IEP available to the parents prior to the meeting.
- Since you are not face to face, periodically remind the team to introduce themselves before speaking.

During an IEP meeting there are several best practices one should consider and implement to foster meaningful parent participation. First, fully consider every suggestion the parents make. It does not mean that the school is going to incorporate them into the IEP; however, the team needs to ensure every comment and suggestion made by the parent is considered. Remember parents do not have veto power over the IEP. The IEP is a consensus document. Negotiation and compromise skills are needed to work toward a consensus when disagreements arise.

Second, fully consider every piece of information the parents bring to the team related to evaluations completed outside of school. An **independent educational evaluation (IEE)** could come from a psychologist, counselor, doctor, or social worker.

Scheduling Best Practices

- Speak to the others from the team that need to be there before you contact the parents. Are there days that are just off-limits for one of the team members?

- Present several dates and times to the parents. Do not state "this is the meeting time"; give a few choices.

- Record all contacts with the parents regarding scheduling. Every call. Every email. Also, note any response from the parents.

- Once the date is confirmed, make sure to send a reminder to the parents (and others) about the time and place for the meeting.

- Send another reminder day of the meeting.

Figure 8.2   Best Practices When Scheduling IEP Team Meetings.

Review the IEE and incorporate relevant parts into the present levels of academic achievement and functional performance (PLAAFP) section of the IEP. This does not mean IEE suggestions need to be fully implemented. As a part of the considerations of the school team, there needs to be clarity about whether the student exhibits behaviors identified in the IEE in the school setting. Be careful rejecting the information from outside the school as the district is now on notice that there is an issue that may need to be addressed.

Third, answer every question the parents have about the program and placement for their child. Make sure to provide timely answers. If you do not know the answer to a question, let the parents know you are seeking information in order to effectively answer the question and will get back to them as soon as possible.

Lastly, it is always best practice to start an IEP meeting with parents by discussing their child. Use the student's name and discuss their strengths. Parents love their children and want what is best for them. Keep the meeting focused on the needs of the student and how special education is about providing educational opportunities for their child.

Overall communication. Parental participation in the IEP process should be a priority. However, it should not stop there. Teachers and administrators should also work during the course of the year to keep parents fully informed about the progress of their child. This includes not only the mandatory reporting of progress at the end of the marking period, but additional periodic updates on activities in the classroom, good behavior commendations, grades on individual assignments, and anything else of note. Work to establish a sense of communication with parents so that the information may flow both ways, and that the parents may reach out to you with questions, concerns, or comments.

Make sure to also respond to questions from parents. If you do not know the answer to their question, work to get the answer—learn and share with others who work with the student but make sure you respond in a timely fashion. Finally, it is all right to say that you do not know the answer to one of their questions, but that you are working to get the information and provide them the answer. Be there for parents and be the point of contact for them before the IEP meeting, during the IEP meeting, and after the IEP meeting. The development of the IEP is just one (although important) part of the process. Make sure parents are involved in the rest of the process as well.

Where can I find more information about parent participation?

Waterford.org. Waterford.org seeks to blend the best aspects of learning science, mentoring relationships, and innovative technologies to form community, school, and home programs that deliver excellence and equity for all learners. At this website, the benefits of parent involvement are discussed: https://www.waterford.org/education/how-parent-involvment-leads-to-student-success/.

Center for Parent Information and Resources (www.parentcenterhub.org). A central "hub" of information and products created for the network of parent centers serving families of children with disabilities. This website provides parent-friendly explanations of IDEA requirements for parental participation. Questions such as *What is prior written notice?* are answered: https://www .parentcenterhub.org/qa2/.

Section 300.322 of IDEA on Parent Participation. Directly access the statutory regulations of IDEA on parent participation at https://sites.ed.gov/idea/regs /b/d/300.322.

Frontline Education (www.frontlineeducation.com). A short video and webpage provide five strategies to improve the IEP process with parent participation. Visit the video and site here: https://www.frontlineeducation.com/blog/ strategies-to-improve-the-iep-process-with-parent-participation/.

Key Terms

Good-faith effort: Sincere and honest effort.

Independent educational evaluation (IEE): An evaluation conducted by a qualified examiner who is not employed by the school district.

Meaningful: A serious, important, or useful quality or purpose.

Predetermination: Fixing, settling, or finalizing in advance.

Professional expertise: A unique set of skills, knowledge, and experiences because of one's profession.

Discussion Questions

1. What are the benefits of meaningful parent participation?
2. Why is predetermination a potential violation of IDEA?
3. What would you do if a parent disagreed with the IEP team's evaluation that their child qualified for special education?
4. What other court cases have impacted the fifth pillar of special education, parent participation?

References

Amanda J. v. Clark County School District, 267 F.3d 877 (9th Cir. 2001).

Doug C. v. Hawaii Department of Education, 720 F.3d 1038, (9th Cir., 2013).

Center for Parent Information & Resources (2017). *Parental rights under IDEA.* Retrieved from https://www.parentcenterhub.org/parental-rights/

Individuals with Disabilities Education Act of 2004, 20 U.S.C. §§ 1400.

Yell, M. L., Katsiyannis, A., & Losinski, M. (2015). Doug C. v. Hawaii Department of Education: Parental participation in IEP development. *Intervention in School and Clinic, 51*(2), 118-121. https://doi.org/10.1177%2F1053451214560894

CHAPTER 9

Procedural Safeguards

> *A core component of IDEA is ensuring parents understand the protections in place for them and their child. If families are not aware of these protections, they are not able to play their role in this collaborative process.*
> Jenifer Cline
> Montana Director of Special Education

The Ffith and Fourteenth Amendments of the U.S. Constitution ensure that no state may deprive any person of "life, liberty, or property, without due process of law." When the Education of All Handicapped Children Act (EAHCA) was passed in 1975, Congress wanted to guarantee educational provisions for students with disabilities and their families were protected under due process principles. The procedural requirements outlined in 1975, and subsequently strengthened through reauthorization of the Individuals with Disabilities Education Act (IDEA), were designed to give parents meaningful participation in their child's special education planning and placement. In addition, Congress premeditated that disagreements between parents and schools about special education services would arise. Therefore, procedures and policies needed to be in place to remedy such disagreement. Although historic exclusion and discrimination of students with disabilities continues to be rectified today, procedural safeguards remain a critical component of IDEA. In this chapter, we will discuss the sixth and final pillar of special education, procedural safeguards (figure 9.1), and answer these essential questions:

1. What are procedural safeguards?
2. How do procedural safeguards relate to free appropriate public education?
3. What regulations and court cases have defined procedural safeguards?
4. Where can I find more information about procedural safeguards?

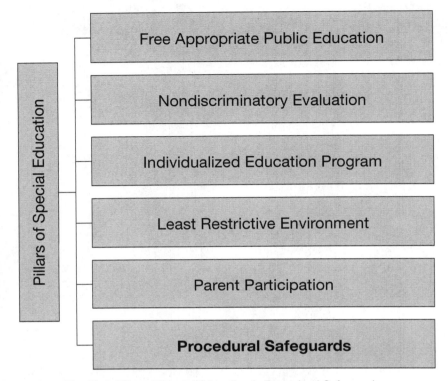

Figure 9.1   The Sixth Pillar of Special Education Is Procedural Safeguards.

What are procedural safeguards?

According to the U.S. Supreme Court, procedural safeguards were established in IDEA to "guarantee parents both an opportunity for meaningful input into all decisions affecting their child's education and the right to seek review of any decisions they think inappropriate" (*Honig v. Doe*, 1988, p. 598). More recently, the U.S. Supreme Court stated "an IEP must be drafted in compliance with a detailed set of procedures. [. . .] These procedures emphasize collaboration among parents and educators and require careful consideration of the child's individual circumstances" (*Endrew F. v. Douglas County School District*, 2017, p. 2). It is evident Congress considered procedural safeguards an important component of IDEA when it was originally passed. Furthermore, state and federal courts have continually upheld the essential nature of procedural safeguards. Within IDEA, procedural safeguards consist of four components: (1) notice and consent requirements, (2) access to relevant records, (3) independent educational evaluation, and (4) dispute resolution procedures (figure 9.2).

   Prior written notice and consent. Parents have the right to receive what is referred to as prior written notice (PWN) before each major decision is made about their child. PWN is a way to keep the parents informed about their rights and the services their child is receiving. Parents have the right to receive PWN in

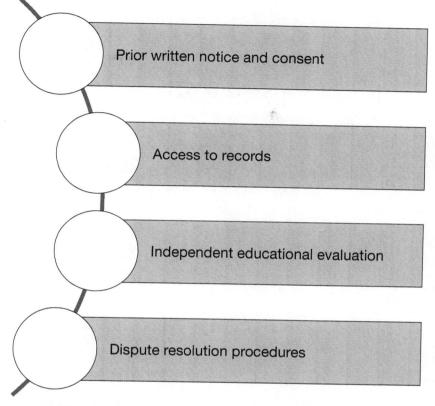

Figure 9.2 Four Components of Procedural Safeguards.

the language they best understand (either spoken or written). As discussed in chapter 8, it is a violation of a parent's participation rights if the information presented to them is not accessible due to language or disability barriers. PWN must be presented to the parent whenever the school (including charter schools) makes a decision about the following components of special education: (a) the child's eligibility for special education and related services, (b) the specific disability the child has, (c) the specific services the child will receive, and (d) how much service will be provided and where. Substantial legal information about a parent's rights related to their child is contained in the procedural safeguards notice. In many states, this is a document that is over thirty pages long and provides a great amount of detail regarding parents' rights and contact numbers for additional information. Figure 9.3 lists the federal regulation's specific requirements for PWN content.

Obtaining parental consent is a key procedural safeguard because it allows the school to carry out the actions proposed in the PWN. As legal guardians of their child, parents must be notified and written consent obtained before a school (a) evaluates the student to determine eligibility for special education,

1. Explanation of all procedural safeguards and how parents can obtain a copy.
2. Description of the action proposed or refused by the school including:
    a. Explanation of why the action is being taken.
    b. Description of options considered.
    c. Reasons why the school proposed or refused to take action.
3. Description of each evaluation procedure used to make decision.
4. Description of other factors relevant to the decision.
5. Description of where parents can obtain information to understand their procedural rights.
6. If not presented in written form, the school must ensure that:
    a. The notice is translated orally or by other means in the parent's native language or other mode of communication.
    b. The parent understands the content of the notice.
    c. There is written evidence that these requirements have been met.

Figure 9.3 Content of Prior Written Notice Requirements under IDEA (IDEA Regulations, 34 C.F.R. § 300.503(b)); Adapted from Yell (2019).

(b) provides special education or related services, (c) reevaluates a student, (d) allows an IEP member to be excused from an IEP meeting, (e) implements an **individualized family service plan (IFSP)** in place of an IEP, and (f) accesses a student's private insurance information (IDEA Regulations, 34, C.F.R. § 300.300 *et seq.*).

The reauthorization of IDEA in 2004 clarified a situation that school personnel were encountering. What happens if a parent refuses to grant consent for what school personnel consider necessary special education services? Or, what if a parent cannot be contacted to provide consent? In these instances, a school may conduct the initial evaluation by applying for mediation and due process procedures. After the initial evaluation, and special education services are deemed necessary, if the parent still refuses to provide consent for services, the school cannot force special education services on the student (Yell, 2019). If the parent denies approval of the program for special education offered by the school, the student is considered a general education student despite the district knowing the student has a disability. The school is no longer liable under IDEA to provide free appropriate public education (FAPE) to that student. In addition, at any time during special education services, a parent may revoke their consent. If revocation occurs, the student is no longer protected under IDEA; the student is considered a general education student, and the school is not liable under IDEA to ensure FAPE.

Access to records. In order for parents to participate as informed members of the IEP team, they have the right to inspect and review all educational records that involve the identification, evaluation, placement, and provision of FAPE of their child (IDEA Regulations, 34, C.F.R. § 300.501 (a)). According to IDEA, schools must comply with a parent's request to review educatio̲ without unnecessary delay (forty-five days or fewer). Furthermore, parents may have a representative (such as an attorney with written permission) inspect and review records on their behalf.

Independent educational evaluations. As noted above, parents have the right to approve or deny whether their child will receive an evaluation for special education. As a part of the evaluation, it is important that parents play a role in the process and their opinion is sought. Each student suspected of having a disability is entitled to an individualized evaluation to help determine their needs and whether those needs indicate the student should receive specialized services. Parents have the right to ask the school to evaluate their child to see if ᵃⁿˢʷᵉ 1 they have a disability and need special education services in school. As discussed in chapter 5, the student must be evaluated using assessments and procedures that are nondiscriminatory. ᵃⁿˢʷᶜ 2

As a check on the evaluation completed by the school district, parents also have the right to seek and obtain an independent educational evaluation (IEE) if they think the school's evaluation was not done properly, or they disagree with the results. Parents can ask the district to pay for the educational evaluation of the child by an approved evaluator who does not work for the school district. Schools that believe their evaluation was appropriate and addressed all the needs of the student may file for a due process hearing seeking an order that they do not have to pay for the IEE. The hearing officer may rule the evaluation performed by the district was appropriate, and therefore the district does not have to pay for the IEE. The parents can still obtain an IEE, but the district does not have to pay for it. The results of the IEE, when shared with the district, must be considered as a part of the student's programming. Results from IEE's do not necessarily dictate what the school should do; rather, they provide the team with an additional data point that will help with special education decisions. ᵃⁿˢʷᵉʳ 3

Dispute resolution procedures. Inevitably, disagreements occur between parents and schools about any number of IDEA procedural or substantive requirements. If parents believe a school has not followed IDEA procedures, or disagree with actions involving the identification, evaluation, or placement of their child, they may file a complaint and follow the dispute resolution mechanisms outlined in IDEA. According to Yell (2019), there are three routes that a parent may pursue when they have a dispute with a school: voluntary mediation, state complaint, and due process hearing. Each state has their own specific dispute resolution procedure (identified in the procedural safeguards notice); however, statutory and federal regulations outline general processes.

Voluntary mediation. Voluntary mediation is the least legally complex procedure and is strongly encouraged as the primary choice for dispute resolution. During mediation, a trained, impartial party facilitates a problem-solving and negotiation process between parties who have reached an impasse (Lake, 2014). The role of the mediator is to facilitate discussions and encourage parties to reach mutually agreeable solutions. The mediator has no authority to impose solutions on either party (Yell, 2019). Mediation sessions should be structured and conducted so that they are less formal and adversarial than other dispute resolution procedures. The Office of Special Education Programs within the Department of Education discourages the presence of attorneys at mediation sessions because attorneys may "have the potential for creating an adversarial atmosphere that may not necessarily be in the best interests of the child" (*Letter to Chief State School Officers*, 2000). If the parent and the school district resolve a dispute through the mediation process, both parties must enter into a legally binding agreement that sets forth the resolution.

State complaint. If voluntary mediation is not successful, or a parent decides to forgo mediation, the parent may file a state complaint for an alleged violation of IDEA. The complaint must include a statement that the school violated a requirement of IDEA, a statement of facts that support the complaint's allegations, and the signature and contact information of the parent. The complaint cannot pertain to an alleged violation more than one year prior to the date that the complaint is received by the state. After receiving a complaint, and state officials determine an investigation is warranted, the state has sixty days to gather relevant information from both parties (i.e., the parents and the school), conduct an on-site investigation, and allow the school to propose a solution. At the conclusion of the investigation, the state will present a ruling which includes detailed findings of facts and conclusions for each allegation in the complaint and a reasoning behind proposed remedies. The state must provide procedures for effective implementation of the final decision. The state does have authority to impose their decision.

Due process hearing. If either party does not agree with the outcome of a voluntary mediation or state complaint, or those options are skipped, parties may request a due process hearing. A due process hearing is the most legally complex procedure because it is **adjudicative**.

The due process hearing is much like a trial in that both parties present facts and argue the legalities of their case in front of a hearing officer (i.e., judge). The hearing officer hears both sides of the dispute, examines legal issues, and settles the dispute (Lake, 2014). In a due process hearing, both parties have the right to:

- Be accompanied and advised by a lawyer and/or persons with special knowledge or training regarding the problems of children with disabilities.
- Present evidence and confront, cross-examine, and require the attendance of witnesses; prohibit the introduction of any evidence at the hearing that has not been disclosed to the other party at least five business days before the hearing.
- Obtain a written, or electronic, word-for-word record of the hearing and findings of facts and decisions.

Due process hearings are where seminal court case decisions originate. If either party does not agree with the due process hearing outcome, the party can appeal the decision up the judicial branch's court system hierarchy.

In 2004, Congress added a **resolution session** to the dispute resolution procedures. Within fifteen calendar days of receiving notice of the due process complaint, and before the due process hearing begins, there must be a resolution meeting with the relevant members of the IEP team who have specific knowledge of the facts identified in the due process complaint. The purpose of the meeting is to discuss the due process complaint as well as facts that form the basis of the complaint, and provide the school an opportunity to resolve the complaint. Schools are not allowed to bring an attorney to a resolution meeting unless the parents bring an attorney. If the school has not resolved the due process complaint to the parent's satisfaction within thirty calendar days of receiving the due process complaint (during the time period for the resolution session), the due process hearing may proceed.

How do procedural safeguards relate to free appropriate public education?

A foundational principle of IDEA is the right of parents to participate in educational decision-making as it relates to their child. The law is very specific about what schools must do procedurally to ensure parents have a strong voice in the entire process of special education (if they wish). Procedural safeguards relate to FAPE by ensuring schools follow proper procedures in planning and delivering FAPE to students with disabilities. Procedural safeguards also provide legal protections and the mechanisms for parents to ensure FAPE for their child. Parents can request mediation, file a state complaint, or request a due process hearing for a broad range of complaints against the school. Some of the most common complaints include:

1. Failure to provide a free appropriate public education (FAPE). Chapter 4 detailed several procedural and substantive components that comprise a denial of FAPE, such as inadequate student progress, lack of shared decision-making with parents, failure to provide sufficient services, and IEPs that do not meet IDEA's requirements.
2. Incomplete or inadequate evaluations that have a problem related to undue delays, limitations in the scope of the evaluation, or lack of appropriate communication with parents.
3. Failure to identify students in a timely manner.
4. Failure to comply with IDEA's child-find requirement that school districts must identify students in their geographic area who may need special education services.
5. IEPs that do not effectively address the student's documented needs.
6. Inappropriate placement when the parents do not agree that the district's proposed placement is appropriate to address their child's disability.
7. Failure to implement a Section 504 plan, or lack of a plan.

What regulations and court cases have defined procedural safeguards?

Winkelman v. Parma City School District (2007). In this U.S. Supreme Court Case, Jeff and Sandee Winkelman claimed that Parma City School District failed to give their son, Jacob, FAPE. Despite the Winkelmans' opposition, the school district planned to place Jacob in a public elementary school. After a preliminary school district hearing affirmed Jacob's placement, the Winkelmans placed Jacob in a private school at their own expense and petitioned a federal district court for reimbursement. The district court ruled in favor of the school district, denying reimbursement for private school tuition. The Winkelmans appealed the decision to the Sixth Circuit Court of Appeals. The Circuit Court dismissed the lawsuit because the Winkelmans were not represented by a lawyer. The Winkelmans argued that according to IDEA procedural safeguards, "any party aggrieved by the findings" of a due process hearing may appeal in a federal court. The Sixth Circuit Court rejected this argument and ruled that non-lawyer parents cannot represent themselves or their child with a disability in federal court.

The Winkelman's appealed the Sixth Circuit Court's ruling to the U.S. Supreme Court. The primary question at stake was, in a lawsuit under IDEA, may a non-lawyer parent of a disabled child argue in federal court either on their own behalf ("pro se") or on behalf of their child? The answer: yes. By a seven–two majority, the Supreme Court reversed the Sixth Circuit decision. The majority opinion stated that parents are afforded procedural safeguard rights under IDEA, which allows them to prosecute IDEA claims on their own behalf. The *Winkelman v. Parma City School District* (2007) case is significant because it affirmed procedural safeguard protections for parents. The decision also emphasized the scope of procedural safeguards, in that IDEA was designed not only to legally protect and educationally benefit a child with a disability but also to legally protect and benefit parents of children with disabilities.

Burlington v. Massachusetts Department of Education (1985). Michael Panico was a student with a diagnosed disability. Following a considerable time of poor performance at his public school, Michael's father and the school discussed changes to his IEP. The school recommended placement in a structured public school program. Michael's father, however, obtained an IEE which recommended placement in a private school program. Michael's father removed his son from public school, enrolled him in the private school, and asked for the school district to pay for tuition. The school district denied tuition payment and filed a due process claim. The hearing officer ruled in favor of Michael's father and required the school to pay tuition. The school appealed the decision to federal court. The federal court ruled the public school placement option for Michael was inappropriate and the private school placement was appropriate. The court demanded the school district pay for tuition, but that it was not required to reimburse Michael's father for the tuition that was paid during the due process proceedings. Michael's father appealed the decision to the First Circuit Court of Appeals. The Circuit Court found the public school placement was also inappropriate and ordered the public school to pay for tuition and reimbursement. The public school district appealed the decision to the Supreme Court.

The *Burlington v. Massachusetts Department of Education* (1985) case addressed two essential questions around procedural safeguards and tuition reimbursement: (1) does IDEA allow for reimbursement for private school tuition and transportation? and (2) does parental rejection of an IEP and placement of the child in a private school, without agreement from the school, deny parents the opportunity for reimbursement? The Supreme Court unanimously ruled that

(1) yes, IDEA guarantees a *free* and *appropriate* education. There may be circumstances where a public school placement option is not considered appropriate. If a public school is not offering an appropriate placement option, parents have the right to unilaterally place their child in an appropriate placement and to not pay tuition for it. The school is responsible for ensuring the child's appropriate education is free. The Supreme Court also ruled that (2) no, parental rejection of an IEP does not bar them from seeking reimbursement after a due process hearing. However, a parent is only entitled to a reimbursement if the public school's placement option is deemed inappropriate. Parents who unilaterally change their child's placement do so at their own financial risk, but they may be reimbursed if the placement is deemed most appropriate by a court.

Where can I find more information about procedural safeguards?

State Department of Education. Each state has a copy of the procedural safeguards written to provide information to parents about their rights. There are subtle changes from state to state (timelines and specific terminology), but the basics of what should be included is the same. Check your state's department of education for a copy of your state's procedural safeguards.

IDEA Basics: Mediation. In this video (6:39), a special education advocate and special education attorney discuss mediation. The content of the video is presented in a manner for parents of children with disabilities. Terminology and concepts are explained in parent-friendly ways. You can access the video here: https://www.youtube.com/watch?v=XWKt8QCSlWI.

IDEA Basics: Due Process. In this video (5:53), a special education advocate and special education attorney discuss due process. The terms and procedures of a due process hearing are discussed in parent-friendly language. You can access the video here: https://www.youtube.com/watch?v=_VQfI0iWZYg.

Wrights Law (www.wrightslaw.com). A comprehensive compilation of resources about various legal topics regarding special education. Browse relevant court cases, articles, and books. To visit a webpage about procedural safeguards and parent notice, follow this link: https://www.wrightslaw.com/info/safgd.in dex.htm.

Key Terms

Adjudicative: The process in which a judge, or arbitrator, rules on a disputed issue.

Individualized family service plan (IFSP): Similar to an individualized education plan (IEP) but for children from birth to three years old.

Resolution session: A mandatory meeting that happens at the start of a due process hearing.

Discussion Questions

1. What do you consider the most important component of procedural safeguards? Why?

2. If you were the teacher of a child with a suspected disability, how would you approach a situation where a parent refuses to consent to an initial evaluation?

3. Why did Congress add the requirement of the resolution session to procedural safeguards?

4. What are some procedural safeguard requirements that are unique to your state's procedural safeguard notice?

5. What are the pros and cons of independent educational evaluations (IEEs)?

References

Burlington v. Massachusetts Department of Education, 471 U.S. 359 (1985).

Endrew F. v. Douglas County School District, 137 S. Ct. 988 (2017).

Honig v. Doe, 479 U.S. 1084 (1988).

Individuals with Disabilities Education Act of 2004, 20 U.S.C. § 1400.

Lake, S. E. (2014). *What do I do when . . . The answer book on special education practice and procedure* (2nd ed.). LRP Publications.

Letter to Chief State School Officers, 33 IDELR 247 (OSEP 2000).

Winkelman v. Parma City School District, 550 U.S. 516 (2007).

Yell, M. L. (2019). *The law and special education* (5th ed.). Pearson Education.

PART III

Additional Issues

CHAPTER 10

Discipline

> *Issues regarding behavior and discipline are the biggest obstacles to students with disabilities receiving education that I see in my practice. If a student is removed from school for disciplinary reasons, it is very difficult for them to receive a free appropriate public education.*
>
> Keith Butler
> *Senior Attorney at Indiana Disability Rights*

Every student deserves a school environment that is safe, supportive, and conducive to teaching and learning. Every teacher also knows that such an environment is neither automatic nor guaranteed. Effective classroom management and discipline are more than simply reacting to misbehavior. Discipline should teach students about the effects of their behavior on others and help them learn to control and manage their own behavior (Yell et al., 2001). Discipline is critical in developing and maintaining a positive and effective classroom environment. Working with students who engage in undesirable behaviors may be one of the hardest parts of being a teacher. Even though all students are to follow the school code, there are different rules for the suspension and expulsion of students with disabilities. Teachers need to know these different rules and understand the purpose behind certain policies and interventions, such as functional behavioral assessments, behavior intervention plans, and behavior rating scales. In this chapter, we will highlight practical tips related to classroom management, discuss the important issue of discipline, and answer these essential questions:

1. What are the differences between disciplining students with disabilities versus students without disabilities?
2. How does discipline relate to free appropriate public education?

3. What regulations and court cases have defined discipline of students with disabilities?
4. How do I ensure procedural and substantive due process regarding discipline?
5. Where can I find more information about disciplining students with disabilities?

What are the differences between disciplining students with disabilities versus students without disabilities?

Before we address the specifics of discipline, especially as it relates to students with disabilities, it is important to discuss the rationale and reasoning behind why schools need to address issues related to discipline in the first place. Students, including students with disabilities, are protected from a deprivation of liberty or property without due process of law by provisions in the Fifth and Fourteenth Amendments to the Constitution. Schools, however, are expected to be safe places for students where they can focus on academic learning and social/emotional growth. Therefore, schools need to have the ability to impose sanctions or penalties for conduct that is deemed to be disruptive. As a result of the need for safety and a calm learning environment, states and local school boards are generally afforded considerable discretion in operating public schools.

A Latin phrase that is pertinent to school authority to discipline students is in loco parentis (i.e., in place of the parent). In loco parentis is an English common law concept under which an individual assumes parental rights, duties, and obligations.

Based on in loco parentis, principals and teachers have the authority to not only teach children, but to guide, correct, and discipline them to accomplish educational objectives (Smith & Yell, 2013). In loco parentis does not completely transfer parental rights to teachers when a child is at school; however, it does allow teachers to maintain an orderly and effective learning environment through reasonable and prudent control of students (Yell, 2019). Regarding disciplinary procedures, in loco parentis authorizes schools to require students to obey reasonable rules and commands and to respect the rights of others. As you might have guessed, the definition of "reasonable" has caused much debate over the years within the courts.

Students with or without disabilities are expected to follow school rules and authority directives to maintain a safe and conducive learning environment. There are no exemptions in this manner for students with disabilities. Osborne and Russo (2009) claimed school administrators often complain that students with disabilities are immune from discipline because of a believed dual standard imposed by the Individuals with Disabilities Education Act (IDEA). This is not true. Students with disabilities are not immune from discipline. IDEA does afford, however, additional procedural and substantive protections for students with disabilities in part because a student's behavior may be related to their disability. A teacher would not reprimand or punish a student who could not see the front of the classroom because of a visual impairment. The teacher would accommodate the student by moving the desk closer to the front of the class, recommend a visual evaluation to obtain corrective lenses, or other actions to assist the student. The same must be true for students with other disabilities (e.g., emotional and behavioral disorders) that may cause inappropriate behaviors. Because students with disabilities are entitled to a free appropriate public education (FAPE), IDEA requires schools to be more proactive when addressing problem behaviors in a student's IEP and follow certain procedural safeguards.

How does discipline relate to free appropriate public education?

Based on the Fifth and Fourteenth Amendments, all students have due process rights. Therefore, all students are afforded procedural due process involving the fairness of methods and procedures used by the school to impose discipline. In addition, all students are afforded substantive due process which involves the reasonableness of the disciplinary process (Valente & Valente, 2005). These due process rights, however, are only for the deprivation of liberty or property. The broad authority of schools to establish rules and procedures means that Fifth and Fourteenth Amendment due process challenges rarely occur. Students with disabilities, however, are afforded additional due process protections under IDEA because they are guaranteed FAPE. The FAPE provision becomes a discipline issue when students with disabilities are suspended or expelled from school, because a student who is not in school cannot receive FAPE.

The U.S. Department of Education has recently made their views clear: The Department of Education

> encourages school environments that are safe, supportive, and conducive to teaching and learning, where educators actively prevent the need for short-term disciplinary removals by actively supporting and responding to behavior. The authority to implement disciplinary removals does not negate their obligation to consider the implications of the child's behavioral needs, and the effects of the use of suspension (and other short-term removals) when ensuring the provision of FAPE. (United States Department of Education, Office of Special Education Programs, 2016, p. 2)

In a seminal U.S. Supreme Court case on discipline (*Goss v. Lopez*, 1975), the court ruled all students had the right to at least minimal due process protections in cases of suspension. The court set a standard that suspensions of ten days or fewer constitute a short suspension. Short-term suspensions require minimal due process protections, such as a written or oral notice of why the suspension is occurring and an opportunity for the student to respond to the charges. The court declared that any suspension over ten days amounts to a long-term suspension and requires additional due process protections, such as a hearing with witnesses and evidence, the right to confront witnesses and present one's own witnesses, and the right to an appeal. For short-term suspensions (ten days or fewer), students with disabilities do not have any additional procedural protections, other than those provided by the *Goss v. Lopez* decision (Norlin, 2007). Any suspension over ten days, whether that is consecutive or cumulative, is considered a **change in placement** for students with disabilities.

IDEA ensures additional due process protections beyond the *Goss v. Lopez* requirements when a change in placement occurs. The IDEA requirements are not meant to shield students with disabilities from long-term suspensions; rather, they are to protect students from unfair or mistaken suspensions.

As discussed in chapter 7 on least restrictive environment (LRE), the educational placement of a student is an individualized educational program (IEP) team decision. The LRE placement decision requires an IEP meeting with parental input and examination of the student's educational needs. Changes in a student's educational placement (especially a change in LRE that is more restrictive) cannot be independently imposed by a school. Therefore, if a suspension of ten consecutive or cumulative days is proposed, the IEP team must meet to discuss whether a change in placement is warranted. If the suspension is considered appropriate, the IEP team must determine how the student's special education and related services will be provided. A suspended student with a disability is still entitled to FAPE.

An additional action that must be taken by the IEP team before changing a student's placement due to a long-term suspension is determining whether the student's inappropriate behavior was a result of their disability. Under Section 504 and the IDEA, students with disabilities cannot be discriminated against. That means a student cannot be subjected to inequitable disciplinary procedures based on their disability. Suspending a student for a behavior that is caused by their disability is discriminatory and illegal. Back to the example of a student with a visual impairment. Imagine a school disciplined a student because they could not complete their math assignment due to an inability to read directions from the back of the classroom. Anyone would consider that preposterous. The same must be true for students with other disabilities that cause undesirable behaviors, even behaviors that violate school rules of conduct. To ensure that the student is not being suspended because of their disability, a **manifestation determination** must be completed by the IEP team, prior to suspension.

According to IDEA (2004), a manifestation determination meeting must occur within ten school days of any decision to change the placement of a child with a disability because of a violation of a code of student conduct. Members of the IEP team must review all relevant information in the student's file, including the student's IEP, any teacher observations, and any relevant information provided by the parents to determine (a) if the conduct in question was caused by, or had a direct and substantial relationship to, the student's disability; or (b) if the conduct in question was the direct result of the school's failure to implement the IEP.

If the meeting determines that the student's behavior is related to their disability, then a long-term suspension is not available. If the student's behavior is not related to their disability, then a long-term suspension and change in placement is available. The IEP team must then determine how a continuation of special education services will be provided in the student's new LRE placement.

In both circumstances, the IEP must conduct a **functional behavioral assessment (FBA)** to identify an explanation of the purpose causing a problem behavior (OSEP questions and answers, 1999). Once the function of behavior has been identified, the IEP team can develop a **behavior intervention plan (BIP)** to address the student's behavioral needs.

To summarize this often unclear aspect of discipline for students with disabilities: students with disabilities are required to follow school rules and can be disciplined for minor infractions just like nondisabled students. Students with disabilities can be suspended short-term, up to ten consecutive or cumulative days, just like nondisabled students. Suspending a student with a disability more than ten consecutive or cumulative days in a school year is considered a change in placement and requires a manifestation determination meeting and IEP team agreement. If a change in placement occurs, FAPE (i.e., a continuation of the student's special education services) must be provided in the student's new placement. Furthermore, the IEP team must conduct an FBA to identify the function of behavior, then develop a BIP to address the problem behavior.

What regulations and court cases have defined discipline of students with disabilities?

Honig v. Doe (1988). In IDEA (2004), there is a provision known as "stay-put." The **stay-put provision** requires students with disabilities to remain in their current LRE placement pending the completion of any review or due process proceedings (unless the child's parents and school authorities agree to removal). In *Honig v. Doe* (1988), the stay-put provision was challenged in court.

John Doe was a student with a disability that caused him difficulty in controlling his impulses. One day, Doe was teased by a peer and responded by physically assaulting the student and breaking a school window. Doe was suspended while the school considered expulsion. Doe filed a lawsuit under IDEA. Another student at a different school, Jack Smith, had a disability that caused behavior problems. Smith engaged in disruptive behaviors and was eventually suspended indefinitely pending a hearing. Smith also filed a lawsuit under IDEA. Since both lawsuits were similar, the two combined their lawsuits into one.

The students asked the court to require their schools to allow them to return based on the stay-put provision in IDEA. The district court agreed with the students that they needed to stay in their current placement during due process and ruled that schools were not allowed to suspend students indefinitely for disability-related misconduct. The school appealed the decision to the Ninth Circuit Court of Appeals where the lower court ruling was upheld. The school then appealed the decision to the Supreme Court.

In a six–two decision the Supreme Court declared yes, the stay-put provision of IDEA prevents a school from indefinitely suspending a student whose disability-related misconduct endangered other students, thus affirming the stay-put provision. The Supreme Court decision did not, however, leave school administrators no options when dealing with dangerous students. The Supreme Court stated that schools can suspend students for up to ten days without a consideration of change in placement. During that ten-day period, school administrators could initiate an IEP meeting and "seek to persuade the child's parents to agree to an interim placement" (*Honig v. Doe*, 1988, p. 605). If a student was truly dangerous and the parents refused a change in placement, the school can immediately seek the aid of the courts. The school can argue that going through IDEA's due process hearing mechanisms to change the student's placement would be too slow, and that the current placement of the student is "substantially likely" to present a danger to others. The court can grant an **injunction** that the stay-put provision be overridden based on the likelihood of danger presented by the student.

Special circumstances. School administrators may unilaterally exclude a student with a disability from school for up to forty-five days for three particular violations:

1. The student brings, possesses, or acquires a weapon at school, on school premises, or at a school function.
2. The student knowingly possesses, uses, or sells illegal drugs, or sells a controlled substance at school, on school premises, or at a school function.
3. The student has inflicted serious bodily injury to another person while at school, on school premises, or at a school function.

If a student is excluded from school for one of these violations, they must be placed in an interim alternative educational setting (IAES) that enables the student to continue to receive their special education services according to their IEP.

How do I ensure procedural and substantive due process regarding discipline?

Procedural due process. Due process procedures for students with discipline issues are not much different from those for students without disabilities, unless a long-term suspension is under consideration. Schools have the authority to discipline students with disabilities just like other students for school code violations (e.g., time-outs, detentions, short-term suspensions, parent–teacher conferences, loss of privileges, etc.). If a school is considering a long-term suspension, the procedural due process for students with disabilities differs from students without disabilities.

Prior to a long-term suspension (ten consecutive or cumulative days), the IEP team must meet to conduct a manifestation determination to evaluate whether the behavior leading to the long-term suspension consideration resulted from the student's disability. If the behavior was related to the student's disability, then a long-term suspension is not an option. The team must conduct an FBA to identify the function of the student's behavior and develop a BIP to address the student's undesirable behavior in the future. Figure 10.1 outlines steps to consider when conducting an FBA.

Substantive due process. Substantively, it can often be difficult to determine whether a student's behavior is related to their disability. Therefore, IDEA is specific about IEP teams being very proactive in addressing student misbehavior.

Step 1	Identify and define the problem behavior in clear, specific measurable terms.
Step 2	Work with IEP team members to identify when the behavior occurs.
Step 3	Collect data on the target behavior by observing the student and using an antecedent, behavior, consequence (ABC) contingency data collection method.
Step 4	Make a determination whether the function of the target behavior is sensory, attention, escape, or tangible.

Figure 10.1 Steps to Conducting a Functional Behavior Assessment (FBA).

Rather than waiting for behavior problems to repeatedly occur or escalate into situations where a long-term suspension is under consideration, IEP teams must develop IEP goals and a BIP to reinforce appropriate behaviors and diminish inappropriate behaviors.

Positive Behavioral Interventions and Support (PBIS) is a set of ideas and tools to proactively improve the behavior of students. At the heart of PBIS is the belief teachers can teach appropriate behavior to all children. Once the function of a student's inappropriate behavior has been identified, interventions can be put in place to replace inappropriate behaviors and reinforce appropriate behaviors. Some important components of PBIS are:

- Start early. Do not wait for problematic behaviors to continue on or escalate.
- Multi-tier support. Match the level of support to the student's individual needs. Some students need minimal support; others need intensive support.
- Use research. Evidence-based, scientifically validated interventions provide the best opportunity for effective behavior change.
- Collect data. The only way to determine if a student is improving is to monitor the student's progress through data collection.
- Use data to make decisions. A data-based decision regarding student response to an intervention is central to PBIS. If the student is not making sufficient progress, adjust the level of support or implement a new evidence-based practice.

Students with disabilities that exhibit problem behaviors that impede their learning, or the learning of others, must have behavioral goals in their IEP (U.S. Department of Education, 2016). The behavior goals must be based on an FBA and include proactive strategies, including PBIS, to address the problem behaviors. Similarly to the academic goals of an IEP, IDEA does not guarantee any specific level of progress toward behavioral goals. As a legal contract, however, the behavioral goals must be addressed in good-faith effort (see chapter 6). If progress monitoring indicates that the interventions implemented to address problem behaviors are not working, the IEP team must try additional interventions. The school must keep trying evidence-based interventions, and documenting those attempts, to execute the student's IEP in good faith. Schools get into legal trouble concerning the substantive due process of a student for discipline when a behavioral problem has gone unidentified or ignored for a substantial period of time. A school that repeatedly suspends a student with a disability but does not convene the IEP team to conduct an FBA, develop a BIP, and add behavior goals to the student's IEP may be subjected to a due process violation of FAPE. Schools are encouraged to collaborate with parents to identify problem behaviors early, proactively implement strategies, progress monitor intervention efficacy, and adjust as needed.

Where can I find more information about disciplining students with disabilities?

Positive Behavioral Interventions & Supports (www.pbis.org). The Center of Positive Behavioral Interventions & Supports is a federally funded website that (a) provides technical assistance to encourage large-scale implementation of PBIS; (b) provides organizational models, demonstrations, dissemination, and evaluation tools needed to implement PBIS with greater depth and fidelity across an extended array of contexts; and (c) extends lessons learned from PBIS implementation to the broader agenda of educational reform.

IDEA Questions and Answers on Discipline. In 2009 the U.S. Department of Education released a document to provide guidance on discipline policies for students with disabilities. Questions such as *Under what circumstances must an IEP Team use FBAs and BIPs?* and *What occurs if there is no agreement on whether a child's behavior was or was not a manifestation of his or her disability?* are answered. The document can be found here: https://www2.ed.gov/policy/speced/guid/idea/discipline-q-a.pdf.

Partnerships for Action, Voices for Empowerment. (www.wapave.org). A resource for parents and educators of students with disabilities. The video (23:27) is for parents of children with disabilities and provides information about legal protections and procedures regarding discipline. The video and other resources can be access here: https://wapave.org/behavior-and-discipline-in-special-education-what-to-do-if-the-school-calls-because-of-a-behavior-incident/.

Key Terms

Behavior intervention plan (BIP): A plan required by IDEA that is based on the results of a functional behavioral assessment and that includes intervention strategies to address a behavior of concern.

Change in placement: When a student's least restrictive environment (LRE) placement is changed.

Functional behavioral assessment (FBA): A process required by IDEA to determine why a student is engaging in a specific behavior.

In loco parentis: A Latin phrase that means "in place of the parent." This common law provides schools with particular authorities to oversee and educate children when at school.

Injunction: A judicial order that compels a party to do or refrain from a specific act.

Manifestation determination: A process required by IDEA to determine whether a student's behavior was related to (i.e., caused by) their disability.

Stay-put provision: A component of IDEA that requires students to remain in their current educational placement pending due process proceedings.

Discussion Questions

1. What are the key differences between disciplining students with and without disabilities?

2. Why is in loco parentis an important concept for education?

3. As a special education teacher, what should you do if one of your students exhibits serious problem behaviors?

4. What is the stay-put provision in IDEA and why was it written into the legislation?

5. How can schools implement positive behavioral interventions and strategies (PBIS)? Why is PBIS important?

References

Goss v. Lopez, 419 U.S. 565 (1975).

Gun-Free Schools Act of 1994 (Pub. L. 103-382, Title I, § 101, October 20, 1994, 198 Stat. 3907).

Honig v. Doe, 56 S.Ct. 27 (1988).

Individuals With Disabilities Education Act, 20 U.S.C. §§ 1400 *et seq.* (2006 & Supp. V. 2011).

Norlin, J. W. (2007). *What do I do when: The answer book on discipline* (4th ed.). LRP Publications.

Osborne, A. G., & Russo, C. J. (2009). *Discipline in special education.* Corwin Press.

OSEP questions and answers. (1999, March 12). *Federal Register, 64*(48), 12,617-12,632.

Rehabilitation Act of 1973, Section 504 Regulations, 34 C.F.R § 104.1.

Smith, S. W., & Yell, M. L. (2013). *Preventing problem behavior in the classroom.* Merrill/Pearson Education.

U.S. Department of Education (2016). *Guidance on discipline. Office of Special Education Programs,* https://www2.ed.gov/policy/gen/guid/school-discipline/files/corpo ral-punishment-dcl-11-22-2016.pdf.

Valente, W. D., & Valente C. (2005). *Law in the schools* (6th ed.). Merrill/Prentice Hall.

Yell, M. L. (2019). *The law and special education* (5th ed.). Pearson Education.

Yell, M. L., Rozalski, M. E., & Drasgow, E. (2001). Disciplining students with disabilities. *Focus on Exceptional Children, 33*(9), 1-20.

CHAPTER 11

Transition and
Related Services

> *The transition services we provide our students lay the foundation for a successful shift from their academic career to their community or workforce career.*
>
> Samantha Leloux
> Special Education Teacher in Delaware

The Individuals with Disabilities Education Act (IDEA) affords early childhood services from birth to age three (Part C) and special education services from age three to age twenty-one—or graduation from high school, whichever comes first (Part B). Some students with disabilities, however, require additional services to benefit from their special education services. These additional services fall under the provision of *related services* and must be provided to ensure a free appropriate public education (FAPE). But what happens to a student with a disability when they graduate from high school or age out of IDEA protections? Transitioning from K–12 schooling to a postsecondary education, life, and career can be an anxiety-inducing experience for both student and parents. Thankfully, clear procedures are outlined within IDEA to address the last few years of a student's education to assist with this transition. In this chapter, we will discuss transition and related services and answer these essential questions:

1. What are transition services?
2. How do transition services relate to free appropriate public education?
3. What regulations and court cases have defined transition services?
4. What are related services?
5. How do related services relate to free appropriate public education?
6. Where can I find more information about transition and related services?

What are transition services?

Special education teachers play a crucial role in helping students with disabilities prepare for adult life. Prior to graduating high school, or turning 21 years old, students with disabilities are protected under IDEA. As we have explored throughout this book, IDEA is a comprehensive, school-based system of supports providing many legal protections for students and their families. Transitioning out of high school means a student with a disability and their family is no longer served under IDEA. The student is entering adulthood and will have legal protections under other disability legislation. As discussed in chapter 3, the ADA of 1990 and Section 504 of the Rehabilitation Act of 1973 provide legal protections for people with disabilities of all ages; however, the level of support is less than that of IDEA. Preparing students and their families to understand these changes while being supported in high school is necessary.

Legally, transition planning is a process that formally takes place over a limited period of time toward the end of high school beginning at age sixteen (some states use a lower age; we will use the federal requirement of sixteen throughout this chapter). However, educators should think about transition planning in elementary, middle, and early high school to pave the way for effective outcomes. The ultimate goal of transition services is to prepare the student for life after school and after IDEA. According to IDEA (2004), transition services are

> a coordinated set of activities for a student, designed within an outcome-oriented process, which promotes movement from school to post-school activities, including postsecondary education, vocational training, integrated employment (including supported employment), continuing and adult education, adult services, independent living, or community participation. The coordinate set of activities shall be based upon the individual student's needs, taking into account the student's preferences and interests, and shall include instruction, community experiences, the development of employment and other post-school adult living objectives, and, when appropriate, acquisition of daily living skills and functional vocational evaluation.

Congress added transition services into IDEA out of a concern that special education students would leave the school setting unprepared for adult life and responsibility (Norlin, 2010). The individualized education program (IEP) for each student with a disability must address transition service requirements beginning not later than the first IEP to be in effect when the child turns sixteen, or younger if determined appropriate by the IEP team, and must be updated annually thereafter. The IEP must include:

1. Appropriate measurable postsecondary goals based upon age-appropriate transition assessments related to training, education, employment, and, where appropriate, independent living skills.
2. The transition services (including courses of study) needed to assist the student with a disability in reaching those goals.

TABLE 11.1 Examples of Postsecondary Transition Goals and Services

Domain	Postsecondary Goal	Transition Service/Activity
Training/education	The student will receive on-the-job training working with children.	The student will participate in the Early Childhood Experience Program at the career center.
Employment	The student will work in the field of technology.	The student will explore two to three colleges that offer either certification or degrees in informational technology.
Independent living	The student will live at home and prepare simple meals and snacks daily.	Student will cook weekly in the classroom to practice cooking a variety of simple meals and snacks.

Specific postsecondary goals and activities will be based upon a student's individual needs. Therefore, courses of study or activities related to meeting appropriate transition goals can vary widely. Table 11.1 provides a list of example goals and activities that meet the domains of training, education, employment, and independent living skills.

How do transition services relate to free appropriate public education?

Transition services have procedural and substantive requirements as they relate to FAPE. According to Lake (2002), four common procedural errors committed by schools are (1) transition services are not addressed in the IEP of a student who is sixteen or older; (2) the school fails to include required transition participants at an IEP meeting; (3) the parents of the student are not informed about the role of transition planning; (4) the transition plan does not include a coordinated set of activities to help the student meet their post-school goals.

Substantively, transition services in an IEP are to (a) infuse a longer-range perspective into the IEP process; (b) assist each student in making a meaningful transition from the school setting to a post-school setting, which could include further education, employment, or independent living; and (c) help students better reach their potential as adults (Prince et al., 2013). To ensure transition services are appropriate under the FAPE requirement, the most critical component is individualization. Each student has unique preferences and educational needs. The courts have been quick to rule that a violation of FAPE has occurred when schools develop minimal or meaningless transition plans.

A recommended approach to developing a substantively compliant transition plan is to look at everything through postsecondary school outcomes.

A post-school outcome goal statement is "generally understood to refer to those goals that a student hopes to achieve after leaving secondary school" (IDEA, 2004). Transition planning should be a student-driven process; therefore, including the student (and parents) in the IEP meeting is paramount. Transition activities and services must go beyond what any student would receive through general education (e.g., career search or college information provided by school counselor). Transition planning can be vague when the student is younger. For example, a transition goal for an eighth-grade student might be: After school, Matthew will work full-time in a career working with cars. However, once Matthew approaches graduation, his transition goal should become more specific. For example, after graduating from high school, Matthew will enroll in ABC automotive technician school and take classes to prepare for a career as a mechanic. Similar to IEP academic goals, transition goals must be specific, measurable, and attainable to be substantively compliant.

What regulations and court cases have defined transition services?

Yankton School District v. Schramm (1995). Tracy Schramm was a high school student at Yankton High. She had cerebral palsy and had been receiving special education services under the orthopedic impairment category since entering public school. Tracy did not have any intellectual or learning disabilities. At the end of Tracy's ninth grade year, she successfully completed adaptive physical education. The Yankton school district did not offer physical education beyond ninth grade. Subsequently, the Yankton school district held an IEP meeting and informed Tracy's parents that she no longer qualified for special education services since she did not need accommodations for physical education. Furthermore, in all transition areas of Tracy's IEP, the school had written "not applicable." Tracy's parents did not agree with the school's decision and filed a due process hearing. Given Tracy's mobility issues, the Schramms wanted her to receive transition services to ease the passage from high school to independent living away from home, especially considering Tracy's desire to attend college. The school argued that Tracy's orthopedic impairment was not affecting her educational performance, and that therefore she did not need special education services.

The lawsuit eventually made its way to the Eighth Circuit Court of Appeals where the justices ruled in favor of Tracy and the Schramm family. The court strongly denounced Yankton school district's minimal and meaningless transition services for Tracy. The ruling emphasized the importance of collaborating with parents and students to comprehensively implement an individualized transition plan.

Jefferson County Board of Education v. Lolita S. (2014). M. S. was a high school student with a learning disability. During an IEP meeting, M. S.'s parents reviewed his IEP and noticed that among other academic goals, the transition goals were not individualized and included **boilerplate** language. In fact, some of the goals included the name of another student, indicating that language was copied and pasted from one IEP to another. There was also no evidence that the school had conducted a transition assessment to develop individualized postsecondary goals and transition services. M. S.'s parents filed a due process hearing alleging a denial of FAPE.

After a hearing officer and district court ruled in favor of M. S., and subsequent appeals by the Jefferson County Board of Education, the Eleventh Circuit Court of Appeals upheld the lower courts' rulings. The Eleventh Circuit Court ruled that a lack of individualized transition planning and programming deprived M. S. of FAPE. In addition, vague language to describe M. S.'s postsecondary goals such as "student will be prepared to participate in postsecondary education" was woefully inadequate.

The courts have consistently held that procedural and substantive violations concerning transition planning and services amount to a denial of FAPE. It is important that transition planning be viewed as an essential component of a student's IEP and not be overlooked. All students will transition out of IDEA protections at some point, and it is imperative schools do their part in helping students better reach their potential as adults.

What are related services?

IDEA (2004) states students with disabilities are qualified to receive special education and related services in order to receive FAPE in their least restrictive environment (LRE). Within previous chapters we have mostly discussed special education services; that is, specially designed instruction to confer educational benefit. Some students, however, may require related services in addition to their special education services. Related services are provided in order for a student with a disability to benefit from special education services. IDEA (2004) defines related services in the following terms:

> Related services means transportation and such developmental, corrective, and other supportive services as are required to assist a child with a disability to benefit from special education, and includes speech-language pathology and audiology services, interpreting services, psychological services, physical and occupational therapy, recreation, including therapeutic recreation, early identification and assessment of disabilities in children, counseling services, including rehabilitation counseling, orientation and mobility services, and medical services for diagnostic or evaluation purposes. Related services also include school health services and school nurse services, social work services in schools, and parent counseling and training.

Federal regulations provide a list of related services, yet the list is illustrative not exhaustive. There are many services that may qualify under the related services provisions of IDEA. The important point to remember is whether the service provides the student greater access to and benefit from special education services. When related services are provided to a student with a disability, the services must be included in the student's IEP and they must be provided at no cost.

Some related services require goals, objectives, and progress monitoring. For example, a student with physical therapy needs will work toward making appropriate progress in light of their circumstances. Other related services, such as transportation to and from school, will not have goals and progress monitoring, but all related services must have specifications in the IEP about (a) when the service will begin, (b) how often it will be provided and for what amount of time, and (c) where it will be provided.

How do related services relate to free appropriate public education?

As a legal provision of IDEA, related services relate to FAPE both procedurally and substantively. Related services are an integral component of an IEP; therefore, all procedural requirements when developing an IEP pertain to related services. The student's evaluation must be comprehensive and explore whether any related services are required. Parents must be included in the IEP meeting discussion about related service needs. If identified and included in a student's IEP, the related services must be implemented as written in the IEP in good-faith effort. Lastly, any changes to a student's related services must be agreed upon at an IEP meeting.

Substantively, related services are provided to compliment the special education services a student receives. Related services can never be provided without accompanying special education services (Pitasky, 2000), meaning that a student must first have special education service needs before related services are considered (Tatgenhorst et al., 2014). The type and extent of service is determined by the IEP team based on the student's individual needs. Similar to other special education services, the IEP team should adhere to the Supreme Court guidance on what constitutes an appropriate education. According to the *Endrew F. v. Douglas County Schools* (2017) ruling, the substantive obligation under IDEA is that schools must offer an IEP reasonably calculated to enable a child to make progress appropriate in light of the child's circumstances. Related services must also substantively follow this guidance.

Irving Independent School District v. Tatro (1984). *Irving Independent School District v. Tatro* (1984) was the first Supreme Court case involving related services. This seminal court case did not necessarily examine the procedural and substantive requirements of related services and FAPE. Rather, this important case explored the term "free" within FAPE and to what extent schools were required to pay for related services.

Amber Tatro was born with the condition spina bifida. Due to this medical condition, Amber had a neurogenic bladder, which essentially prevented her from properly emptying her bladder on her own. To prevent further injury to Amber's kidneys, her doctor prescribed a clean intermittent catheterization (CIC) procedure to be completed every three to four hours. Based on Amber's disability of spina bifida, she qualified for special education services and was provided an IEP. Her IEP, however, did not include the CIC procedure as a related service. Amber's parents petitioned the school to include the CIC procedure as a related service because without the procedure Amber could not access her special education services. After unsuccessfully pursuing a due process hearing, the Tatros appealed to a federal district court where they also lost the lawsuit. The district court ruled that CIC was a medical procedure. Medical procedures do not fall within the related service mandate of IDEA. The Tatros filed an appeal to the Fifth Circuit Court of Appeals where the lower decision was reversed in favor of the Tatros. The Fifth Circuit Court ruled that the CIC procedure was a supportive (related) service and not a medical service. Therefore, the school must include the CIC procedure in Amber's IEP free of charge. The Irving Independent School District appealed the decision to the Supreme Court.

The essential question needed to be answered by the Supreme Court was: what constitutes a related service (required under IDEA) versus a medical service (not required under IDEA)? The Supreme Court ruled in favor of the Tatros that CIC was a related service, and to provide guidance for lower courts, the Supreme Court stated that a particular service is covered under IDEA as a related service if three criteria are met: (1) the student must be IDEA eligible, (2) the service must be necessary to assist the student to benefit from special education, and (3) the service must be performed by a nurse or other qualified person (services performed by a physician are excluded).

The final criterion is known as the "**bright-line test**" and relates to whether a service is considered supportive or medical. According to the Supreme Court, if a physician has to provide the service, the school is not responsible for paying and providing the service. If a non-physician can provide the service, then the school is responsible for providing the service. Although Amber's need for regular CIC was medical in nature, the procedure was actually fairly simple and easily performed by a qualified school nurse. Since a physician was not required to perform the CIC, then the procedure was a related service and required by IDEA to ensure FAPE for Amber.

Where can I find more information about transition service and related services?

Individuals with Disabilities Education Act. In section 300.34 of the IDEA legislation, the terms and services of related services are defined and described. Examining the legislation will provide an illustrative list of related services: https://sites.ed.gov/idea/regs/b/a/300.34.

Department of Education. The office of special education and rehabilitative services has created a transition guide to provide clarity on requirements under the law pertaining to transition services and postsecondary education and employment for students with disabilities. The guide can be found here: https://www2.ed.gov/about/offices/list/osers/transition/products/postsecondary-transition-guide-august-2020.pdf.

National Collaborative on Workforce and Disability (www.ncwd-youth .info). A resource that assists states and local workforce development systems to better serve youth with disabilities.

National Technical Assistance Center on Transition (www.transitionta
.org). NTACT hosts "toolkits" of resources on a variety of topics, related to
secondary education and services for students with disabilities and the capacity-
building associated with improving such education and services. These toolkits
provide an overview and then step-by-step guidance and resources on the specific topic.

The IRIS Center (www.iris.peabody.vanderbilt.edu). The IRIS Center
is a national center dedicated to improving education outcomes for all children through the use of effective evidence-based practices and interventions.
The IRIS center has multiple modules, case studies, and activities for professional development in transition and related services.

Key Terms

Boilerplate: Written text that can be used repeatedly without significant changes.
Bright-line test: A clearly stated and easy-to-follow rule.

Discussion Questions

1. Why are transition and related services important provisions in IDEA?
2. What should IEP teams do to ensure legally compliant transition services?
3. What additional court cases have challenged the bright-line test regarding related services that was established by the Supreme Court?
4. Why is it important for a student with a disability and their family to prepare for transitioning?
5. What are some differences between IDEA and ADA?

References

Individuals with Disabilities Education Act of 2004, 20 U.S.C. §§ 1400.
Irving Independent School District v. Tatro, 468 U.S. 883 (1984).
Jefferson County Bd. of Educ. v. Lolita S. ex rel. M.S., 64 IDELR 34 (11th Cir. 2014).
Lake, S. E. (2002). *IEP procedural errors: Lessons learned, mistakes to avoid*. LRP
    Publications.
Norlin, J. W. (2010). *Postsecondary transition services: An IDEA compliance guide for
    IEP teams*. LRP Publications.
Pitasky, V. M. (2000). *The complete OSEP handbook*. LRP Publications.
Prince, A. M., Katsiyannis, A., & Farmer, J. (2013). Postsecondary transition under
    IDEA 2004: A legal update. *Intervention in School and Clinic, 48*(5), 286-293.
Tatgenhorst, A., Norlin, J. W., & Gorn, S. (2014). *What do I do when . . . The answer
    book on special education law*. (6th ed.). LRP Publications.

CHAPTER 12

Confidentiality in Special Education

> *Confidentiality is important in special education because it is a promise between staff, students, and families that there will be protection related to their education.*
>
> *Angie Gilbert*
> *Special Education Teacher in Idaho*

Prior to 1974, parental access to educational records was often denied. Schools were reluctant to grant access because it was time-consuming and costly, and increased liability by allowing public scrutiny (Yell, 2019). Furthermore, student records were often made available to third parties without consideration of student confidentiality (McCarthy et al., 2013). Congress recognized this problem and set out to address concerns regarding confidentiality with the Family Educational Rights and Privacy Act of 1974 (FERPA). Shortly after, when the Education of All Handicapped Children Act of 1975 was passed, the confidentiality provisions of FERPA were incorporated into the law. Confidentiality of student information is now a very important component of the Individuals with Disabilities Education Act (IDEA). Rightly so, there has been a lot of legislation, regulation, and case law related to ensuring education professionals know their responsibility toward students' files, records, and identifying information. Confidentiality was especially important during the COVID-19 pandemic as guidance related to FERPA was one of the first items the U.S. Department of Education wrote about (U.S. Department of Education, 2020). In this chapter, we will discuss confidentiality in special education and answer these essential questions:

1. What is confidentiality?
2. What laws are related to confidentiality?
3. How does confidentiality relate to free appropriate public education?

4. What regulations and court cases have defined confidentiality for students with disabilities?
5. Where can I find more information about confidentiality?

What is confidentiality?

The basic principle of confidentiality is about privacy and respecting someone's wishes. As mentioned in the introduction, prior to 1974, parents were often not allowed to access their child's educational records, nor were those records maintained as confidential to **third parties**.

There was an obvious problem with the system when a parent could not see their child's record, but a stranger could. Congress wanted to amend this problem, so James Buckley of New York introduced a law, known as the Buckley amendment, to (a) ensure that parents and students would have access to their educational records, and (b) protect students' right to privacy by not releasing records without consent (Bathon et al., 2017). Confidentiality in special education is, therefore, two-pronged. It gives parents the right to access their child's educational records, and it gives the student a right to record privacy.

What are the specific laws related to confidentiality?

The Family Educational and Privacy Rights Act (FERPA) is the primary source of law that determines confidentiality in education for all students, not just students with disabilities. FERPA consists of five components (figure 12.1). Any public or private school that receives federal financial assistance must adhere to the provisions of FERPA. There are five basic requirements:

1. School districts must establish written policies regarding student records and inform parents of their rights under FERPA annually.
2. Parents are guaranteed access to their children's educational records.
3. Parents have the right to challenge the accuracy of the records.
4. Disclosure of these records to third parties without parental consent is prohibited.
5. Parents may file complaints under FERPA regarding a school's failure to comply with the law.

Since FERPA is dealing with the confidentiality of educational records, it is important that we define educational records. Educational records are all files, documents, and other materials that contain personally identifiable information directly related to a student and that are maintained by the school or by a person acting for the school (Yell, 2019). It is helpful to identify educational records that are not covered by FERPA as well. Personal notes that are made by a teacher about a specific student are not considered educational records, as long as those notes are not revealed to other persons, except substitutes. Records of law enforcement activities (e.g., school police officers) are not

Coverage

- Any educational agency that receives any type of federal funding or directs and controls an educational institution.

Purpose

- To allow parents access to educational records relating to their children. To prohibit disclosure of education records to third parties unless the school obtains prior written parental consent for such disclosure, or an exception to the consent requirement applies.

Notices

- School districts must notify parents of students annually regarding their rights under FERPA.

Amendments

- School must set up procedures to allow parents to request amendments to educational records, as well as a hearing process, in case the parents disagree with a school's decision to not amend a certain record.

Enforcements

- The Department of Education has set up the Family Policy Compliance Office (FPCO) and the Office of Administrative Law Judges to enforce compliance with FERPA, review and investigate complaints, and, in the case of FPCO, provide technical assistance regarding compliance with FERPA.

Figure 12.1   Five Components of the Family Educational Rights and Privacy Act (FERPA).

considered educational records as long as they are maintained for law enforcement purposes. Also, directory information such as name, address, date of birth, telephone number, and email address are not considered educational records.

Regarding students with disabilities, IDEA has determined that the definition of educational records includes (a) individualized education programs (IEPs); (b) school evaluations, medical evaluations, independent educational evaluations, and any other documents that pertain to a student's educational performance; (c) recordings of IEP meetings; (d) transcripts of due process hearings; (e) complaints filed with the school; and (f) correspondence and investigative findings regarding a complaint if they contain personally identifiable information.

FERPA v. HIPAA. The Health Insurance Portability and Accountability Act (HIPAA) of 1996 is often confused with FERPA. Enacted in 1996, HIPAA works to improve the effectiveness of the health care system through the establishment of national standards for electronic health care transactions but also to protect the privacy and security of individually identifiable health information. HIPAA requires the protection of individuals' health (i.e., medical) records and other identifiable health information by requiring appropriate safeguards to protect privacy. When a school provides health care to students, it has responsibilities under HIPAA. The main difference, therefore, between FERPA and HIPAA is that FERPA pertains to educational records while HIPAA pertains to health records.

How does confidentiality relate to free appropriate public education?

The first essential aspect of FERPA is privacy. Educational records that have personally identifying information (e.g., a student's name) are almost always going to be protected under FERPA. It is best practice, therefore, to secure written consent before disclosing any record with personally identifiable information or remove all personally identifiable information from the record before disclosure.

One major exception to FERPA is that educational records can be disclosed to educational personnel with legitimate educational interests. Most eligible students with disabilities receive most of their education in general education classrooms (National Center for Education Statistics, 2020). Historically, general education teachers did not know the specifics of special education services provided to students. This posed a particular problem in middle and high schools where students often have multiple teachers throughout the day. Although one general education teacher is required to be on a student's IEP team and attend IEP meetings, what about all of the other teachers? If teachers do not know what is in a student's IEP, they cannot provide services, accommodations, or modification. Failing to implement an IEP and provide services as agreed upon is a clear violation of FAPE.

A student's IEP, therefore, can and should be shared with all of the student's teachers (including paraprofessionals). To be careful with a student's IEP privacy, many schools provide a summary of the student's IEP with forms like "IEP at a Glance."

The summary outlines specific personnel responsibilities so that the IEP is implemented as written in all settings. Providing a summary of the student's IEP to teachers on a need-to-know basis creates a layer of privacy protection for the student and goes above and beyond to ensure FERPA compliance. Teachers who receive IEPs at a glance, however, should still have access to the full IEP if they need additional information. They should also be able to schedule time(s) to meet with the special education teacher(s) or case manager when additional questions arise.

The second essential aspect of FERPA, parental access to educational records, directly relates to FAPE. In chapter 8, we discussed the special education pillar of parental participation. A key component of parental participation is that parents are meaningfully involved in the planning and progress monitoring of their child's IEP. Parents that do not have access to their child's educational records would not be able to meaningfully participate. The right of parents to access their child's educational records affords them the opportunity to participate in the decision-making process of their child's special education services as an informed member.

What regulations and court cases have defined confidentiality for students with disabilities?

Owasso Independent School District v. Falvo (2002). There has only been one U.S. Supreme Court case on student privacy and confidentiality. The case did not address the sharing of student records outside of school or with outside agencies but did address the sharing of students' grades within a classroom. In *Owasso Independent School District v. Falvo* (2002), Kristja Falvo asked the Owasso Independent School District to ban peer grading, or the practice of allowing students to score each other's tests, papers, and assignments because it embarrassed her children. Apparently, students had to exchange papers and grade them according to the teacher's instructions, and then report scores either aloud or in private. Although students could report grades in private to the teacher, at least one other student knew their grade. The parent believed the graded paper counted as an educational record and fell under the guidelines of FERPA. The parent felt this practice violated the privacy rules of FERPA because confidential educational records were being released to others without the specific written consent of the parent. When the school district declined to stop peer grading, the parent filed a lawsuit against the school district claiming that peer grading violated FERPA. The Owasso Independent School District asserted that educational records were only those that were part of a student's permanent record or file, not scores from individual papers or assignments. The central question to the *Owasso Independent School District v. Falvo* (2002) case was, does the practice of peer grading violate FERPA?

In a unanimous ruling, the Supreme Court said no, peer grading does not violate FERPA. The Supreme Court noted that peer grading is an educational experience that teachers and schools are within their power to select. The Supreme Court reasoned that peer-graded items do not constitute educational records, stating, "Student graders only handle assignments for a few moments as the teacher calls out the answers. It is fanciful to say they maintain the papers in the same way the registrar maintains a student's folder in a permanent file" (*Owasso Independent School District v. Falvo*, 2002). In addition, the ruling opinion reasoned that each student grader did not meet the FERPA definition of a "person acting for an educational institution." The Supreme Court did clarify, however, that once those grades go into a permanent gradebook that is maintained by the teacher, then those grades become educational records under FERPA.

34 C.F.R. Part 99. As discussed in chapter 1, regulatory laws provide clarification and guidance on the implementation of statutory laws. Regulatory law 34 C.F.R. Part 99 provides comprehensive explanations of FERPA statutory law (Electronic Code of Federal Regulations, 2020). The regulations are divided into five subparts:

- Subpart A – General.
- Subpart B – What are the rights of inspection and review of education records?
- Subpart C – What are the procedures for amending education records?
- Subpart D – May an educational agency or institution disclose personally identifiable information from education records?
- Subpart E – What are the enforcement procedures?

Under each subpart are several questions such as *How can a parent or eligible student request amendment of the student's education records?* and *Where are complaints filed?* Each subpart and sub-question of the regulations are answered by providing relevant FERPA statutory law quotes. 34 C.F.R. Part 99 is a valuable resource for families, students, and educational institutions to best understand and adhere to FERPA provisions.

Based on federal regulations and other lower court rulings, some important tips to remember when dealing with confidentiality are:

1. Directory information that is generally not deemed an invasion of privacy (e.g., name, email, date of birth) is not considered confidential. Parents can, however, opt out of directory information listings.
2. There is no difference between providing a copy of an educational record and orally disseminating information contained in that record.
3. Parents have the right to inspect any educational record that is kept on their child.
4. Parents can only access information related to their own child, not others, without permission from the other parents.
5. Parents can request to have their child's educational records amended if they find errors.
6. Schools need to regularly inform parents of their rights under FERPA.
7. Schools need to ensure they have a signature from a parent before they release any confidential information.
8. School can disclose educational records to members of the staff who have a legitimate reason to know about the educational interest of the student.
9. Schools can disclose educational records to other schools if the student is already in attendance at the new school.
10. Schools must maintain a record of parties obtaining access to education records each time records are accessed or disclosed. The record must include the party's name, the date of access, and the purpose for which the party is allowed to access the records.

Where can I find more information about confidentiality?

U.S. Department of Education. For further reading, please see the U.S. Department of Education Frequently Asked Questions regarding FERPA.

The document covers nine questions related to the implementation of services for students and the release of information to others. The document can be found at https://www2.ed.gov/policy/gen/guid/fpco/faq.html.

Educators are also recommended to see the Parents' Guide to the Family Educational Rights and Privacy Act: Rights Regarding Children's Education where questions are answered like *Who else gets to see my child's educational records?* You can find this website here: https://www2.ed.gov/policy/gen/guid/fpco/brochures/parents.html.

Protecting Student Privacy. A comprehensive resource provided by the U.S. Department of Education that houses guidance documents, training materials, policy letters, and other resources dedicated to protecting student privacy. You can access the website here: https://studentprivacy.ed.gov/resources.

Key Terms

IEP at a glance: An abbreviated document that provides quick reference to a student's IEP.

Third party: A person or group besides the two primarily involved in a situation.

Discussion Questions

1. Why is it important that parents of children with disabilities have access to their child's educational records?
2. Why is it important that teachers of a student with a disability know the content of that student's IEP?
3. What are some best practices a school can implement to ensure FERPA is not violated?
4. Why are special education teachers generally more concerned with FERPA violations than general education teachers?
5. Explore 34 C.F.R. Part 99 and answer this question about FERPA: *Under what conditions is prior consent not required to disclose information?*

References

Bathon, J., Gooden, J. S., & Plenty, J. A. (2017). Student record. In J. R. Decker, M. M. Lewis, E. A. Shaver, A. E. Blankenship-Know, & M. A. Paige (Eds.). *The principal's legal handbook* (6th ed.), pp. 103-116. Education Law Association.

Electronic Code of Federal Regulations. (2020). Retrieved from https://www.ecfr.gov/cgi-bin/text-idx?tpl=/ecfrbrowse/Title34/34cfr99_main_02.tpl

Family Educational Rights and Privacy Act, 20 U.S.C. § 1232g (1974).

Individuals with Disabilities Education Act of 2004, 20 U.S.C. §§ 1400.

McCarthy, M. M., Cambron-McCabe, N. H., & Eckes, S. E. (2013). *Public school law: Teachers' and students' rights* (7th ed.). Merrill/Pearson Education.

National Center for Educational Statistics. (2020). The condition of education: Students with disabilities. *U.S. Department of Education.* Retrieved from https://nces.ed.gov/programs/coe/indicator_cgg.asp#:~:text=In%202018%E2%80%9319%2C%20the%20number,percent%20had%20specific%20learning%20disabilities.

Owasso Independent School District v. Falvo 534 U.S. 426 (2002).

US Department of Education. (2020). *Student Privacy Policy Office.* Retrieved from https://studentprivacy.ed.gov/sites/default/files/resource_document/file/FERPA%20and%20Coronavirus%20Frequently%20Asked%20Questions_0.pdf

Yell, M. L. (2019). *The law and special education* (5th ed.). Pearson Education.

Key Terms Every Special Educator Needs to Know

504 Plan: The 504 Plan is a plan developed for students who have disabilities but do not require special education services. The plan ensures access to education and services.

Academic achievement gaps: Disparities in academic performance between groups of students.

Academically: Related to learning in core subject areas, for example, reading, writing, and math.

Accommodations: Curricular adaptations that compensate for learners' weaknesses without modifying the curriculum.

Adaptations: Changes in educational environments that allow students with disabilities to participate in inclusive environments by compensating for their weaknesses.

Adequate yearly progress (AYP): The amount of yearly improvement each Title I school and district are expected to make in order to enable low-achieving children to meet high performance levels expected of all children.

Adjudicative: The process in which a judge, or arbitrator, rules on a disputed issue.

Annual review (AR): The yearly meeting of the individualized education program (IEP) team.

Appropriate instruction: Scientific and evidence-based instruction.

Assistive technology (AT): Technology used by individuals with disabilities to assist with functions that might be difficult. Walkers, wheelchairs, screen readers, and magnifying devices are all considered assistive technology.

Attention Deficit/Hyperactivity Disorder (AD/HD): A condition where students have difficulty paying attention and sitting still. Children with AD/HD are sometimes eligible for special education services under IDEA's "other health impairment" disability category.

Autism: A developmental disability significantly affecting verbal and nonverbal communication and social interaction, usually evident before age three, and which adversely affects a child's educational performance.

Baseline: Data regarding a student's current level of performance.

Behavior intervention plan (BIP): A plan required by IDEA that is based on the results of a functional behavioral assessment and that includes intervention strategies to address a behavior of concern.

Behavior plan: A written course for what to do to prevent challenging behavior and what to do when it occurs. A behavior plan should specify a reinforcement and punishment system as well as who is in charge of making revisions, and when the team will meet to discuss updates to the plan.

Behavior support plan (BSP): A proactive action plan to address behavior that is impeding the learning of a student or that of others in their classroom.

Boilerplate: Written text that can be used repeatedly without significant changes.

Bright-line test: A clearly stated and easy-to-follow rule.

Change in placement: When a student's least restrictive environment (LRE) placement is changed.

Child find: A program, mandated by IDEA, that requires states to continuously search for and evaluate children who may have a disability.

Class-action: A type of lawsuit where one of the parties is a group of people who are represented collectively by a member of that group.

Comparable public education: An education of equivalence to nondisabled peers. Does not have to be an exact replication of education but must be comparable.

Compulsory: Required by law; obligatory.

Constituents: The people whom politicians represent from their electing district or state.

Continuum of placements: The range of educational placement settings where a student's IEP can be implemented from least restrictive (general education classroom) to most restrictive (residential hospital/institution).

Controlling authority: Authority from higher courts over lower courts in their jurisdiction.

Court of Appeals: A court tasked with determining whether or not the law was applied correctly in the trial court.

Deaf–hard of hearing (DOHH): A hearing impairment that is so severe that the child is impaired in processing linguistic information through hearing, with or without amplification.

Defendant: A person, company, or institution that is being accused of a crime.

De minimis: A Latin expression meaning "about minimal things." De minimis educational benefit is slightly more than no educational benefit.

Developmental delay (DD): A delay in one or more of the following areas of childhood development: cognitive development, physical development (including vision and hearing), communication development, social and/or emotional development and adaptive development (including eating skills, dressing and toileting skills, and other areas of personal responsibility).

Disadvantaged: Students from impoverished families.

Discrepancy model: Determination of a learning disability by comparing IQ and academic achievement.

Due process hearing: Similar to a courtroom trial where both sides of a dispute can present evidence, call witnesses, and make legal arguments. A hearing officer or judge oversees the trial and makes a judgment.

Early intervention (EI): Services for at-risk children from birth to their third birthdays, as mandated by the Individuals with Disabilities Education Act (IDEA).

Efficacy: Effectiveness or ability to accomplish the intended goal.

Electorate: People in a country who are entitled to vote.

Emotional or behavioral disturbance (EBD): A condition exhibiting one or more specific emotional and/or behavioral difficulties over a long period of time and to a marked degree, which adversely affects educational performance.

Expenditures: The amount of money spent.

Fidelity: The extent to which delivery of an intervention adheres to the protocol or program model originally developed.

Founders: The writers of the U.S. Constitution.

Free Appropriate Public Education (FAPE): The education to which every student is entitled under IDEA. Every student is entitled to an education that is appropriate for their unique needs and that is provided at no costs to the parents.

Functional behavioral assessment (FBA): A process required by IDEA to determine why a student is engaging in a specific behavior.

Functionally: Related to a student's ability in regard to activities of daily living, for example, self-care, daily living, and work-related behaviors.

Good-faith effort: Sincere and honest effort.

Hearing impairment: An impairment in hearing, whether permanent or fluctuating, that adversely affects a child's educational performance.

IEP at a glance: An abbreviated document that provides quick reference to a student's IEP.

IEP team: The team of qualified professionals made up of the parent, special education teacher, interpreter of test data, district representative, and general education teacher at a minimum. This group makes decisions related to the instructional program of an eligible child, including placement and services provided.

In loco parentis: A Latin phrase that means "in place of the parent." This common law provides schools particular authorities to oversee and educate children when at school.

Inclusion: An educational philosophy that students with a disability should be educated alongside their nondisabled peers with supports and services.

Independent educational evaluation (IEE): An evaluation conducted by a qualified examiner who is not employed by the school district.

Individualized: Specific and unique to one's circumstances.

Individualized education program (IEP): A legal document that defines special education services between the school district and the parents.

Individualized family service plan (IFSP): Similar to an individualized education plan (IEP) but for children from birth to three years old.

Individuals with Disabilities Education Act (IDEA): A law that guarantees educational rights to all students with disabilities and makes it illegal for school districts to refuse to educate a student based on their disability.

Informed consent: The signed consent of a parent that describes what the parent is consenting to; informed consent must be obtained before a district assesses, makes a revision to, continues, or stops service of a child's program.

Injunction: A judicial order that compels a party to do or refrain from a specific act.

Intellectual disability (ID): Significantly subaverage general intellectual functioning, existing simultaneously with deficits in adaptive behavior and manifested during the developmental period, that adversely affects a child's educational performance.

Intelligence quotient (IQ): One of the measures used to determine eligibility for special education services.

Interagency programs: Programs that bring together professionals from various disciplines such as occupational therapy, speech pathology, medical services, and counseling.

Interventions: Sets of teaching procedures used by educators to help students who are struggling with a skill or lesson succeed in the classroom.

Jurisdiction: Authority granted within a defined field of responsibility.

Least restrictive environment (LRE): A mandate in IDEA that students with disabilities should be educated to the maximum extent appropriate with their nondisabled peers.

Legal precedent: Rulings that establish legal principle and are applied to other cases with similar facts.

Level of educational benefit: The degree to which one is expected to demonstrate functional and/or academic progress.

Life skills classroom: A special education classroom for students with more severe disabilities. A modified curriculum focuses on functional, adaptive, social, and academic skills specific to students' individual needs.

Mainstreaming: An outdated term representing an educational philosophy that students with disabilities should spend time with their nondisabled peers for a portion of the day (i.e. recess, nonacademic classes, lunch).

Manifestation determination: A process required by IDEA to determine whether a student's behavior was related to (i.e., caused by) their disability.

Meaningful: A serious, important, or useful quality or purpose.

Modifications: Curricular adaptations that compensate for learners' weaknesses by changing or lowering expectations or standards.

Multidisciplinary team: A group of individuals from multiple disciplines (e.g., special education teacher, general education teacher, psychologist, principal) who evaluate a student for special education and collaborate to create an individualized education program.

Multiple disabilities: Simultaneous impairments (such as intellectual disability-blindness, intellectual disability-orthopedic impairment, etc.), the combination of which causes such severe educational needs that they cannot be accommodated in a special education program solely for one of the impairments. The term does not include deaf-blindness.

Native language: The first language of an individual. A school district is required to evaluate a student in their native language, or document proficiency in English, before they can identify the student as having a disability and provide special education services.

Nondiscriminatory: Not biased for or against any individual or group of students.

Objective: Defined; clear-cut; based on facts not opinions.

Occupational therapist (OT): A professional who treats patients with injuries, illnesses, or disabilities through the therapeutic use of everyday activities.

Orthopedic impairment (OI): Physical disabilities which could affect the academic process.

Other health impairment (OHI): A disability category under IDEA where students with health-related conditions may qualify for special education. Some disabilities include attention deficit/hyperactivity disorder, diabetes, epilepsy, heart conditions, hemophilia, lead poisoning, leukemia, nephritis, rheumatic fever, sickle cell anemia, and Tourette syndrome.

Overrepresentation: Representation of a group in a category that exceeds expectation for that group.

Parliamentary procedures: Processes by which the legislative branch drafts legislation, debates the legislation, and votes to approve or disprove the legislation.

Performance deficit: A social or academic skills deficit in which a student understands a particular skill but fails to implement it consistently.

Performance-based tests: Evaluations, such as the Woodcock Johnson or the Wechsler Individual Achievement Test (WIAT), that are used to help determine a child's eligibility for special education services.

Persuasive authority: Written opinions by lower courts or courts of other jurisdictions that a judge is not obligated to follow but which may help inform the judge's decision.

Physical therapist (PT): Professionals who help people who have injuries or illnesses improve their movement and manage their pain.

Pillar of special education: Major principle of IDEA that focuses on students' rights and the responsibilities of public schools to students with disabilities.

Plaintiff: A person, company, or institution that initiates a lawsuit.

Positive behavior support (PBS): An approach to eliminating challenging behaviors and replacing them with prosocial skills.

Predetermination: Fixing, settling, or finalizing in advance.

Present levels: A component of an individualized education program (IEP) that defines a student's strengths and weaknesses, current levels of academic achievement, and current levels of functional performance.

Procedural rights: Procedures that must be followed to ensure special education rights, as outlined in IDEA, are provided.

Professional expertise: A unique set of skills, knowledge, and experiences because of one's profession.

Progress monitoring: Scheduled data collection to monitor a student's progress toward a goal.

Provisions: A required directive within a law to protect the interests of one or both parties in a contract.

Reasonable accommodations: Accommodations that provide opportunities for students with disabilities in comparison to their nondisabled peers without excessive financial or administrative burdens.

Reauthorization: A renewal of the authority, legal power, or right of.

Regulations: Instructions written by the executive branch that provide direction on how to implement and enforce laws passed by Congress.

Related services: Transportation and such developmental, corrective, and other supportive services as are required to help a child with a disability benefit from special education.

Resolution session: A mandatory meeting that happens at the start of a due process hearing.

Resource room: A special education classroom for students with less severe disabilities. Specialized instruction and academic remediation are provided for students' individual needs. Students with disabilities attend a resource room for only part of the school day or a few times a week.

Response to intervention: Determination of a learning disability by measuring a student's response to increased levels of academic support.

Rigorous: Extremely thorough, exhaustive, and accurate.

Scientifically based research: Systematic and empirical research that (a) uses observation or experiments with rigorous data analyses to test the stated hypotheses, (b) relies on measurements or observational methods that provide valid data across evaluators and observers, and (c) has been accepted by a peer-reviewed journal or approved by a panel of independent experts through a comparatively rigorous, objective, and scientific review.

Seminal: Strongly influencing later developments.

Specially designed instruction (SDI): Adapting the content, methodology, or delivery of instruction to address the unique needs of a student and ensure access to the general education curriculum.

Specific learning disability (SLD): A disorder in one or more of the basic psychological processes involved in understanding or in using spoken or written language, and that may manifest itself in an imperfect ability to listen, think, speak, read, write, spell, or do mathematical calculations. Specific learning disabilities include conditions such as perceptual disabilities, brain injury, minimal brain dysfunction, dyslexia, and developmental aphasia. The term does not include learning problems that are primarily the result of visual, hearing, or motor disabilities, of intellectual disability, of emotional disturbance, or of environmental, cultural, or economic disadvantage.

Speech or language impairment: A communication disorder such as stuttering, impaired articulation, a language impairment, or a voice impairment that adversely affects a child's educational performance.

Speech-language pathologist: A professional who diagnoses and treats communication and swallowing disorders.

Spending clause: "The Congress shall have power to lay and collect taxes, duties, imposts and excises, to pay the debts and provide for the common defense and general welfare of the United States [. . .]" Article 1, Section 8, Clause 1.

Stakeholders: Persons with an interest in something regarding a particular outcome.

Standardized: Calibrated in a manner to allow comparisons of relative performance of one individual to a group of individuals.

Stay-put provision: A component of IDEA that requires students to remain in their current educational placement pending due process proceedings.

Subjective: Ambiguous; not easily defined; interpreted with feelings and opinions.

Substantive rights: Protections of the content and quality of educational services.

Supersedes: Takes the place of what was previously in authority; a new priority.

Supplementary aids and services: Aids, services, and other supports that are provided in general education classes, other education-related settings, and extracurricular and nonacademic settings, and that enable students with disabilities to be educated with nondisabled students to the maximum extent appropriate.

Third party: A person or group besides the two primarily involved in a situation.

Transition planning: Planning to promote successful movement from high school to post-school activities, such as postsecondary education, vocational training, employment, adult services, independent living, and community participation.

Transition/transition plan: A plan for a student who will turn sixteen (or younger in some states) and must have a transition goal and plan outlining how they will move to life beyond high school.

Traumatic brain injury: An acquired injury to the brain caused by an external physical force, resulting in total or partial functional disability or psychosocial impairment, or both, that adversely affects a child's educational performance.

Trial court: A court of law where cases are first tried with a fact-finding process and a jury to provide a verdict based on the strength of the plaintiff's or defendant's case.

Triennial review: A review every three years to ensure that a student needs special education.

Veto: A constitutional right to reject a decision or proposal made by a law-making body.

Visual impairment: An impairment in vision that, even with correction, adversely affects a child's educational performance. The term includes both partial sight and blindness.

Zero reject: A component of the child-find provision in IDEA that ensures no child can be denied a free appropriate public education regardless of severity of disability.

Index